LINDA

W9-CPE-119

Acclaim for BECOMING SINGLE

'So often books like this can be patronising and simplistic and don't tell you much that is new. BECOMING SINGLE actually makes good reading . . . the personal stories liberally dotted throughout the book are well-edited, short, relevant and interesting.'
New Woman (Australia)

HAMISH KEITH was born in Dunedin in 1936 and was educated in Christchurch. He now lives in Auckland. Married in 1962, he divorced in 1982. Originally an art historian and curator at the Auckland City Art Gallery, he became a freelance writer and broadcaster in 1970. A frequent contributor of newspaper and magazine columns, his published works include *Being Single and Happy*, *The Bayswater Brasserie Book of Food*, *New Zealand Painting 1840–1890*, *An Introduction to New Zealand Painting*, *New Zealand Yesterdays*, *Images of Early New Zealand* and *Above Auckland*, as well as a number of television plays and documentaries.

Wellington-born Dinah Bradley works as a part-time physiotherapist, writer, photographer, women's health activist, TV researcher, wife and mother. Having been at the eye of the storm in many marriage break-ups, including a sister, brother, in-laws, and several close friends, divorce has never held much appeal for her. Feeling at close quarters the pain and chaos of families in distress made the experience of co-writing this book – collecting women's stories with the detached eye of an outsider – a positive, albeit harrowing one. Her published works include *Grandma's Teeth*, a picture book for children, and *The Hazards of Heavy Breathing*, a book on hyperventilation syndrome.

Becoming Single

How to Survive When a Relationship Ends

Hamish Keith

with

Dinah Bradley

POCKET
BOOKS

New York London Toronto Sydney Tokyo Singapore

First published in Australasia in 1991
by Simon & Schuster Australia
First published in Great Britain by Pocket Books, 1993
An imprint of Simon & Schuster Ltd
A Paramount Communications Company

Copyright © 1991 Hamish Keith

Adapted for UK law by Imogen Burton

This book is copyright under the Berne Convention.
No reproduction without permission.
All rights reserved.

Simon & Schuster Ltd
West Garden Place
Kendal Street
London W2 2AQ

Simon & Schuster of Australia Pty Ltd
Sydney

A CIP catalogue record for this book is available from the British Library

ISBN 0-671-71581-X

Typeset in Goudy Old Style and Helvetica Light by
Hewer Text Composition Services, Edinburgh
Printed and bound in Great Britain by
Harper*Collins* Manufacturing, Glasgow

Contents

Foreword

Hamish Keith and Dinah Bradley provide a personal account of an event and its processes that almost one out of three couples will experience at least once in a lifetime.

All research indicates that the best way of healing the wounds of separation is to be patient with yourself and allow yourself and your partner to go through the process. This book gives a commonsense guide to the experience and practical problems that separated persons face. It draws on psychological, medical, legal and importantly folklore sources to describe the experiences and problems associated with separation. In exploring these, the authors work towards a positive adjustment and an end result of individual growth and a sense of individual worth.

Jan Williams
Executive Director
Marriage Guidance New South Wales

Introduction

This book was conceived when I was in the midst of the process of separating after eighteen years of marriage. I was completely overwhelmed by what was happening to me. I couldn't explain it. I didn't have the faintest idea how to cope. Looking back I realise just how badly I handled most of it. One thing, though, was crystal clear – there had to be a better way.

In its early stages the book itself seemed an impossible task. It was only when I was able, in my mind, to shift its focus from its sad beginnings as 'Breaking Up' to the more positive 'Becoming Single' that writing it became at all possible. At that stage I gathered together all the earlier threads and with the energetic collaboration of Dinah Bradley rewove them into this book.

This is a book written for newly separated persons by two non-specialists – one who has been through the experience and the other who has been closely supportive of friends who have. The book draws on medical, legal, psychological, and other specialist sources, but it is basically a commonsense resource book designed to describe the immediate experience of separation and its associated practical problems, and to define some simple strategies to help the newly separated cope.

It also defines the experience in positive terms. Separation is painful. It will produce rage, grief and anxiety; it can produce practical and economic problems; it might produce illness and stress symptoms; but it is also a chance to grow as a person, to set out on a challenging and exciting new life, to find or build new skills, to make new friends and to find and explore a range of personal freedoms not always available within a relationship.

In writing this book we have drawn on the direct experience of dozens of separated men and women. Our gratitude to them is immense. Without their willingness to share their pains and joys, hopes and fears honestly and frankly, our account of the process of becoming single would have little real dimension. At the same time, we were astonished at the consistency of reaction and response our contributors expressed and were encouraged by that. In our belief the experience has powerful common threads that can be understood, and by understanding and positive interpretation it can become a springboard to change and growth for the individuals involved.

We would particularly like to record our considerable debt to Carroll du Chateau for the generous access she gave us to her earlier research.

Hamish Keith
Auckland

CHAPTER ONE

Breaking Up

I just couldn't believe it. We were driving home and he suddenly stopped the car and said in a very quiet voice "I'm sorry, really sorry, but there's this other woman. I'm in love with her and I'm leaving." I thought my heart was going to stop. There was this great roaring silence and his words just got bigger and bigger inside my head. No warning. Out of the blue everything just fell apart. Even now, months later, I can't go up that bit of the street without feeling sick or frightened. I'm never going to forget that moment. It's going to be burnt into my brain forever like a grainy photograph of some dreadful crime.

We had a dreadful row the night before and I had pushed her out of the house. She went to her sister's and rang from there the next morning to say that she was leaving. I begged her to stay — said I would leave instead, move into the spare room — anything that came into my head to give us some time, but none of it worked. I felt numb, frozen with fear and apprehension. It took me a long time to go back in my mind to that moment, but I knew I would have to face it eventually, if only to know how much better I was.

. . . .

Even in our relatively pragmatic times, love, engagements and weddings are presented in an aura of romantic happiness and approval. Two people have chosen each other for a lifetime's commitment. Family and friends show their support in various celebrations, culminating in the wedding. The ceremony, gifts, speeches and confetti all symbolise the romantic choice and contract that has been cemented between the happy couple.

There is no confetti at the separation.

You were chosen and now you have been unchosen.

Your future, once so full of loving promise, now seems a frightening vacuum.

There is no ceremony or ritual to help you through what has suddenly happened to you. Breaking up is a foreign land and everything about it seems strange. You are jolted awake from your dream or nightmare to find yourself in a place populated almost entirely by well-meaning strangers with disturbingly familiar faces.

When you are part of something you feel protected and powerful. When you are pushed or jump out of that circle the immediate feelings of disorientation and powerlessness can be terrifying.

But this is the worst you are going to feel.

This is the only part of the emotional journey you have begun over which you will not have much control. Once you are through this first, frightening stage, things are going to get progressively better. Recovery may be fast or slow – the speed it happens will depend a great deal on how well you organise yourself to cope – but recover you will.

I seemed to be in a daze. It felt like standing in a high wind, being buffeted and burnt and not quite being able to hear anything. Moving was an effort, gravity seemed to have doubled. I couldn't focus or concentrate. I was bereft.

I made up my mind that however badly I felt I would force myself to work. Luckily I had an interesting project going but, even with that, the horror of what had happened to me was there all the time – an awful feeling of apprehension in the pit of my stomach. I decided to pretend it was only something physical that would pass – I even took aspirin for it to fool my body too – and while I was working that seemed to help. The minute I had my mind back to myself, though, nothing at all would make it go away or deaden it.

As bruised and rejected as you might feel, you just have to push past those feelings and pull together all your inner resources. You need to have faith in yourself – a firm belief that you are eventually going to come out the other side of this experience. You also need to have faith in your friends and in your family.

Breaking up sends a shudder through every part of your life. Psychologists rank it along with bereavement as one of the most stressful human experiences. But unhappily, as a society, we have not yet developed any ritual or instinctive support systems to help cope with the grief of a separation.

The changes set in train by breaking up can affect your social status, your relationships with family, close friends and children, your income and, almost instantly, your self-image. Many of these changes will be inevitable. Some of them can be avoided or modified by your own awareness of them. Not all of them will necessarily be bad. In many cases the changes thrust on a person by separation can represent a new freedom and a whole new set of possibilities.

At the very least, each change can be seen as a challenge and if you accept challenges as opportunities, the whole painful process could leave you better off in the end. This is not just a straw for you to clutch at. A large number of men and women who have gone through a separation and divorce and have successfully coped with their grief have found that they are stronger as a result.

There are other opportunities, too, beyond emotional strengths, which can come through successfully coping with that experience. We come to them later in this book.

Breaking up might be the end of a relationship, but it is the beginning of something new too. It is also likely to be one of the most traumatic experiences you will ever have. Your frames of reference are entirely new and unknown. You need to make demands on your emotional and physical energy quite unlike any you have made before – and this at a time when you are probably at your lowest ebb.

It was beyond reason why I felt so inconsolable – it was quite out of proportion – I was better off without him. But the grief welled up from deep down inside. I know my friends thought I was going overboard, but it was like a great cleansing madness.

The grief you feel may well have tentacles reaching back to childhood and unresolved events of your earlier life. The separation may be a trigger for a whole set of disturbing experiences you had suppressed or refused to acknowledge. If these have come to the surface along with the pain of the break-up, then it is wisest to acknowledge them for what they are. Knowing exactly why you are feeling bad is a pretty important part of coping.

Don't feel guilty about your misery. Don't wallow in it either, but give it a good, wholehearted expression and once it is on the surface, then let yourself know what it is all about. Try to identify all the things which make you feel sorry for yourself. You may be surprised to find just what it is you have been hanging on to, hurting for, or resenting.

In this first onslaught of your emotions, you are likely to be given the maximum amount of licence by your friends and family. Without drowning them in your misery, make the most of their sympathy, but make sure you do it in a positive way, not just by repeating the same miserable cries.

Some people will go to the most extraordinary lengths, exhausting themselves and the people around them, rather than sit down and face up to what is happening. These are the sort of people who use up all the oxygen in a room, drink all the booze and wring the last drop of energy out of their friends, leaving everyone exhausted.

Mostly their energy and passion is spent on assigning blame, wallowing in guilt, bouts of blind rage, or asking, over and over again, questions they have no intention of answering. Of course it is hard to avoid some of that, but if you are going to use your friends to help you, then listen to what they have to say. If they offer comfort and advice, then accept it as a way of moving on and not as an excuse to stay trapped in your misery.

Generally speaking, this first phase is harder for men to express than for women. Most men are adept at burying their emotions and sidetracking their feelings. The separated man going through this stage of the break-up may be tempted to retreat into an excessive workload or life in the fast lane. The danger of putting one's life into full throttle as an antidote to emotional pain is that a major breakdown in health, induced by stress, may bring you to a full stop.

Another common response for men is to search immediately for a new partner, without properly coming to terms with themselves or with the end of the last relationship. This is a great way to set themselves and some new person up for yet another emotional disaster.

It's seven years now since my first husband and I split and he still seems stuck in the first phase. I think it's because like most men the heart-to-mouth link has been blurred from early on – they seem to have the heart-to-cock link fairly well together, but getting their feelings moving in the other direction and out into the open is just too hard for most of them.

There will be a whole lot of questions about the future crowding in with your emotions. Try to put most of those aside. Some you may have to deal with – like children, housing and that kind of thing – but even many of those will have long-term implications that you will need to deal with in a calmer, less passionate frame of mind.

Deal with the immediate things first. Your own self-image will have taken a battering. Soothing that particular hurt is a sensible priority, since your self-esteem is going to be a valuable asset in going through the process to come.

The buzz word everyone said to me was self-esteem. 'You're a terrific person', they said. 'Where's your self-esteem?' But it was my self-image that I needed to see to. I didn't believe for a moment that I was a terrific person . . . How come my old man had fallen in love with someone else? I didn't see how anyone could love me and I sure as hell didn't think I was worth much to anyone. I carried on for months being a real pain in the bum, radiating gloom. There was a constant and wearying battle in my head between self-esteem and self-contempt. But self-image is looking at yourself in a bigger sense – turning yourself round to look outside again.

After a couple of weeks I 'came out'. Scared as hell and shaking, I got myself dressed up and went to a small farewell party for a friend travelling overseas. It was an incredible experience. I felt raw and weak and quite useless socially, as if I had to learn some of the rules all over again. I also felt as if I was sticking out like a sore thumb and that everyone could see how exposed I was. Couldn't touch the alcohol – I was sure I'd fall over if I had a sip. I sat quietly in a corner and went home early.

As a start you have to face up to the reality of what has happened. There will be times when that will seem a near impossibility and you will be seduced away from the reality by a whole lot of 'if only' scenarios. There may be some comfort in rewriting the past in your mind, or in refusing to believe what has actually happened, but that will be very temporary.

The hard fact is that you have been dumped. It might have come as a horrifying surprise, or you might have been expecting it for months or years. Now it has happened and accepting that is the first real step you can take towards having some control over your future.

This is a good time to take stock of your assets. One technique is to draw up a balance sheet. At the top write the title of this book *Becoming Single*. Then make a list of all the things you can think of that are on the credit side of that. You can be as silly and flippant as you like, but think of all the things you can do and be as a single person that you couldn't do as one half of a couple.

Now you can list all the debits – all the things you think you might find impossible to do on your own. You might be surprised at how many things on the debit side can be crossed off with a bit of hard questioning.

Now, having cut your teeth on the cans and can'ts, start another double column entry. This time write down all the things you like about yourself and all the things you know you are good at. Now the hard bit: write down all the things you don't like about yourself – be brutally honest – and all the things you know you can't do well or avoid doing.

This debit column might cause you some pain, but once you have done it, start asking the same hard questions you asked of the other debit column. First of all you can cross out all the things you have no control over – age and height are two obvious ones if you have put them on the list – then underline all the things you could work on — like weight, smoking and fitness for instance.

Again you may be pleasantly surprised to end up with a remarkably short list of negatives. If you have a very close friend you feel confident about, let him or her have a hack at the list too and negotiate a few more things either right off the list or into the 'able to change' category.

In your present frame of mind, this sort of exercise might seem a bit jokey or trivial, but it is worth trying at least. At the very worst you can just get impatient with the authors of this book. At best you will have drawn up a blueprint for your entry into the next phase of the process — recovery.

Stepping out from the shelter of a marriage or long-term relationship means having to expose yourself to a lot of new situations, or situations you have lost the habit of. It doesn't matter if you make mistakes and have occasional spills. After all, you only have yourself to answer to, and the occasional feeling of foolishness will be more than offset by the real feelings of achievement that coping with the new will give you. The more open and honest you are with yourself, the easier these confrontations will seem.

We were like two young trees when we were married. Growing so close to each other our limbs intertwined. When he split from me it was as though bits of me had been torn off and I had this pale exposed side that hadn't grown like the rest of me. The wounds took some time to heal, but the catching up of growth has taken a lot longer. The hurt side withered at first in the bright harsh light . . . couldn't take the heat, but in my own time I am becoming whole again.

Business commitments or children may mean that some separating couples will need to maintain contact. For one or both these meetings might make recovery from the break-up harder. If contact is stressful then it is important to keep meetings to a minimum until you are stronger. Let your ex know that you don't wish to meet any more often than is absolutely necessary and avoid the temptation to turn a practical necessity into a slanging match or a pain-filled battleground.

If possible use family and friends as an initial buffer. Remember, though, that this may also make problems for them. In any case avoid using such meetings to score points or raise false hopes.

What I found hard to deal with was the fact that I still loved this man and at the same time hated him with every fibre in my body. He had lied to me, been a total bastard, and yet I'd still get a charge hearing his voice on the phone. I hated myself for that. I felt he was exploiting my leftover love for him. He'd come round to see the kids and stay and we always ended up screwing and then he'd go back to his new woman. I even got sick pleasure for a while in the reversed role and me being the 'other woman'. It might seem wrong, but there is no 'right' or 'wrong' way to recovery, is there? You have to chart your own course until the ground gets familiar again.

I forget the reason she came round, but we had a drink or two and began to talk about our feelings as if we were talking about two other people. It surprised me to discover that she still felt sexual feelings for me and that one of her regrets was that we would no longer be lovers. I very nearly asked her to make love there and then, but in my heart I knew that she was just expressing her regrets and not offering anything for now or the future. I am glad she said it – it made me feel better about myself – and I am also glad I was cool enough to avoid a painful rebuff.

During this first impact of separation the stress on your mind and body can be colossal. It is common to attract all sorts of minor infections and ailments. It is important to adopt certain strategies to help keep yourself healthy.

In the first few weepy weeks most people want to show their hurt. It is a natural response and it is healthy to do so. One of the greatest causes of stress and stress-related illness is suppressing emotions. But unduly prolonging your misery can also set you up for a physical decline.

Depression becomes a habit. The miserable person in the driving seat somewhere in the front of your head can shut out more useful emotions. Of course you feel miserable – you have every reason to – and you feel depressed. What could be more depressing than breaking up with someone who had become an essential element in your life and your view of the future?

Perhaps you even have reasons to feel guilty too. These emotions are an essential part of the mixture that makes up a feeling person. But no single one of them should be allowed to take control.

I finally got some professional help. I had been sceptical of counselling and was, right up to when the counsellor began. But bit by bit I saw a glimmer of hope – I realised that I was clinging on to my misery to punish myself and maybe to punish my wife as well. I had let misery blot out everything else to the point where I was making myself quite seriously ill.

Depression can set up a vicious circle. Because you feel depressed you don't eat properly or get enough exercise and this physical neglect feeds your depression. (Failure to thrive is common in unloved babies.) Many authorities cite poor nutrition as the greatest cause of stress. Add smoking and drinking to that and you have a recipe for potential long-term damage.

Some simple strategies will help you get control of your life again and minimise the potential for illness that your misery has created.

• Take vitamins C and B complex and magnesium. Most health shops stock stress remedies which are a balance of these and sometimes include other trace elements or ginseng. These basic vitamins and trace elements are rapidly depleted in your system in what is called the 'Fright-Flight-Fight' aspect of fear and stress. Lower levels of vitamins C and B complex reduce tolerance to stress even more. Magnesium deficiencies have been shown to contribute to heartbeat irregularities. (A substantial majority of heart attacks are preceded by severe emotional stress.)

• Make sure your diet is balanced. Avoid getting into a junk food habit and if you are caring for children avoid imposing one on them. Children are an excellent motivation for maintaining good eating habits. They are also sometimes the worst temptation to settle for the local chippy or takeaway bar instead of a balanced meal.

● Get some physical exercise. If you are not given to sports, then get in the habit of going for regular long walks. If you can, take up a sport – or pursue one you already play. Whacking games such as squash or tennis are a good release.

● Learn some basic relaxation techniques and learn to recognise tension areas. A lot of stress gets caught up in the trapezius muscle – the big flat, trapezium-shaped muscle that lies across your back from the base of the skull to the top of your shoulder blades. Neck and arm exercises can relax and loosen tension areas in this muscle – too much tension built up in it can produce a classic bad back and headaches.

● Deep breathing and tension-freeing exercises can make you feel incredibly refreshed. There is a whole range of these – from the kind mothers learn at pre-natal classes to the meditation-inducing techniques of yoga. Your local library will almost certainly have a host of works on this subject.

● Make sure you get adequate sleep and rest. This may be difficult, but physical tiredness is a good prelude to sound sleep. Don't panic if your sleep patterns are muddled. Everyone varies and it is important not to try to force sleep on yourself. If you do wake early or can't get to sleep, give your mind something more nourishing to feed on than misery – read, listen to music, or get up and do something around the house.

● Be very cautious about chemical happiness. Tranquilisers and sleeping tablets might provide some immediate relief, but their long-term physical and emotional effects can be far worse than the problem they were meant to treat. Try herbal teas as an alternative. Health shops carry a range of these and they are usually labelled with their soothing or reviving characteristics.

My sister dragged me off to a naturopath. I was a bit doubtful, but my GP wasn't helping much. He just said 'Time heals all wounds' and gave me some calm-me-down pills that made me feel slightly fuzzy and out of focus. But at the naturopath's I had a wonderful massage. 'Ten years of tension in these shoulders', she said. She gave me a list of vitamins and homeopathic remedies to buy. The alternative health lot look after all of you. I mean I wasn't really sick, but I did need help.

On the hidden agenda of your mental state there will probably be a lot of fears about the future and about becoming single again. As soon as you can, flush these out into the open and come to terms with them. Many will be justified, some can be easily overcome or can be seen to be only very short-term things. All of them are fears other people have and have coped with.

My worst fear was fear of poverty. I'd had a poor childhood and I knew what it is like to envy and want. I married a man who could provide and I gave up my career when we had kids — we had the traditional two — and I made a career out of being a wife and mother. I sewed, cooked, gardened and entertained — it was a great show for a few years.

Then one day my husband said 'What about me?' I was appalled at his perception of me as having a good time all day while he slaved to provide the money. My perception was that I worked my guts out to provide a fabulous environment for him and his bloody kids. We were both so dissatisfied. We did dreadful things to each other. Rowed all the time. And he walked out. My greatest terror is real. My children are poor — like I was.

My worst fear was the loss of family. But one day at the doctor's I saw a magazine article which asked 'Think of the families you know. What is normal now?' It listed: a couple with his and hers and their child; grandparents raising a grandchild; a couple sharing everything but a marriage licence; a divorced woman and her children; a single woman and her adopted child. Nuclear families aren't so super-normal nowadays and a family is a relationship not a number.

My worst fear was loneliness, but I found when I left the marriage and had to meet and mix with people it improved my social confidence hugely. I realised I had been desperately lonely when I was married.

My worst fears were surrendering the sense of respectability that goes with marriage. I made the mistake of trying to keep up with married friends when we separated, where, of course, I didn't really fit in anymore. Gradually I found the alternative culture of the newly single.

I was just terrified of change. And things today change so bloody fast. I was the perfect nineteenth century husband. I was afraid of having no past. My whole adult life had been spent with one woman and two children and it seemed to have gone with them. My stories, the things that were important to me, the tastes I had formed, the reasons I had for my beliefs — who could know them now? It was like being struck dumb.

Your separation may have struck like a thunderbolt, or you may have seen it coming from a long way off. Whichever, it is likely to be one of the most stressful experiences you are likely to encounter in your life. It is important, from the very beginning, to come to terms with the reality of what is happening to you — a reality that millions before you have faced and that millions are going to face.

There is a wealth of other people's experience and wisdom to help you through. Do not be afraid to look for help, to ask for help or to accept help when it is offered. Learn to tell the difference between advice and opinion. A lot of well-meaning friends will think they are helping by reinforcing your prejudices or fuelling your rage; you are better off ignoring that kind of 'help'.

Put your own well-being first. If you are going to crack up you will be of little use to your family or anyone else who may have to depend on you. At the same time don't pretend your misery isn't real or try to suppress or deny your feelings.

Your separation is going to be painful, but being hurt won't kill you and you can tolerate more pain than you think. Just keep in your mind that pain is the currency of emotional transactions and if you are not prepared to take the risks of being hurt you are not likely to have real and worthwhile relationships.

The process you have started on – whether you chose it or not – has a beginning, a middle and an end. In the next chapter we will look more closely at the stages of that process.

Becoming single is a challenge, it can be an adventure and it is a situation full of new opportunities. The sooner you let your depression lift the more clearly you will appreciate the positive things about your new state.

I remember being a student for a year in a foreign country. For the first three months I was in a state of absolute exhaustion, learning the language and ways of the society. Then I started to get the feel of the place and get confident. I felt like that when my marriage ended – finding the whole new ways of behaving, thinking, coping with the stress. I felt roughly the same as I had as a young student.

It was fantastic finding a whole subculture of separated and single-again people leading such interesting lives. I started going to ballroom dancing classes . . . I used to adore dancing. I can't tell you how wonderful it was, dancing and hearing music again. I started riding again and teaching at the local pony club. At 57 I'm single, busy, and seem to have a whole new life.

CHAPTER TWO

Fear and Loathing

About six months after my wife and I had split I re-met an old friend whose husband had died at about the same time. I could see straight away that her feelings and mine were the same, but they weren't being dealt with in the same way. We would sit around saying what a great guy he had been, when we both knew that like most of us he was only partly a good guy and had often been a swine. When we came to talk about my wife the whole thing shifted. We didn't talk about the good things but only about the negative ones. Here I was grieving and in pain – all for some thoroughly unpleasant person. It seemed crazy, but my grief was just s real as hers. One day I upset her by saying that I was worse off than her since Peter wasn't still around making a nuisance of himself!

. . . .

If you have been dumped (and sometimes even if it was you who did the dumping) your feelings are going to be exactly the same as the grief you would go through if your partner had died. You **are** grieving. Grief is normal. Only, the grief you feel on breaking up does not attract the same social rituals and understanding that a death would. Your friends might find it hard to share your feelings or respond to their depth. They would have had no problem if you and they had gone through a funeral service.

The first thing you have to come to terms with is that grief is not just some nasty parcel of pain and fear and rage. It is a process. It has a beginning, a middle and, you will be delighted to know, an end. It is a natural process, the first of many on the way to recovery. The best way to get through the grieving process is to know that you will be better off by doing so.

It is a painful process and one that most people would do anything to avoid, but you have gone through a major change in your life and grieving is inevitable. People who shadow-box with their grief, or who try to hide from it and avoid the hefty adjustments that are necessary to come to terms with their loss, can often end up in a chronic groove of black depression or physical ill health.

All I know is that emotional feelings make mincemeat of any intellectual ideas you might have to cope with a separation. I'd always been a calm, thinky sort of person, but I was totally overwhelmed and actually quite stunned by the power of my grief, anger and anxiety.

The safety valves have to blow. Just hang on to the truth that while that blowout will probably begin as a piercing shriek, it doesn't go on for ever and sooner or later it will end as a gentle flutter.

It is not a bad idea to tackle this business of mythologising your errant partner. Draw up a kind of balance sheet (just like the one you did for yourself) of all the things you are going to miss and all the things you are glad to be rid of. You can cheat a bit if you like and make the 'won't miss' list a little longer. But remember you are grieving for someone, or a relationship, you loved and your pain would be a bit unreal if you blotted that out entirely.

If marriages are made in heaven, separation comes straight out of hell. I hate to think of what I was like when we first split. For the first few weeks I didn't sleep night or day. I'd ring him late at night. I threw bricks through their window. I pulled all the plants out of their garden. I'd try to sleep, but I started hallucinating – I kept seeing his body next to me in our bed. He loved someone else.

The beginning of grief is frightening, volatile and emotional.

The middle is dark, depressing and full of regret, guilt and blame.

The end is reached when you achieve a sense of detachment from the lost love and old way of living. There will still be some pain and of course there will be scars, but this is a phase when you are suddenly filled with ideas about the future. A door will seem to have opened. The little grey person who seemed to be driving your head will have retreated to the corners where little grey people should lurk. Everyone who successfully works through his or her grief comes up stronger for the experience.

It is work. You have to do it. No-one else can or will.

Grasping those three truths is the beginning of your journey through to the other side.

It was more than a year later, almost a year and a half. I was sitting in this restaurant with two women friends – two gay women – and I felt really good about things. I thought 'Isn't this funny. Here I am, a bloke, with the couple I feel closest to' – and they really had helped me all the way – 'and they're a gay couple.' I thought how marvellous that my life could change so much and then I just burst into tears. The very first tears for my bust-up marriage. It wasn't that sort of hurt bubbling – just tears pouring down my cheeks. I felt really good about it and so did my friends and then we saw this other guy at the next table just staring at me in horror – his fork frozen halfway to his face. And we all started to laugh. Me just sitting there crying and laughing and feeling good. And I thought 'If only I could have cried before', but I suppose I wasn't really ready for tears before. I think it was then I was really sure for the first time that I was going to get over it. I still had a long way to go and it's lucky that I didn't know then just how far. But at least I was well on the way.

One of the first things I did when he finally left was to rearrange my bedroom. The kids let me borrow their goldfish bowl. Fish are soothing to watch. They really slow your sobbing down. I festooned my place with living things – flowers, pot plants and ferns to cover the gaps where he had taken his things away.

I think that allowing myself to grieve was the single most important thing I did – accompanied by a bit of weeping and rocking and carrying on. I'd grieve for me, for her, for us, for the good times together, for the loss of the family unit, for the kids, for the loss of a certain social acceptability.

During a couple of really bad ones I indulged myself a bit by deciding during the evening that I'd take the next day off work, giving me the whole night to weep and wail. My new flatmates came to recognise this. 'I'm grieving', I'd say. They'd nod wisely, letting me carry on. I'm very glad now that I allowed these emotions to flood out because they were an important stage I had to go through. Missing a few days off work was a small price.

The reaction to the obvious losses involved in separation goes through three quite distinct stages.

The first is SHOCK/DENIAL, which might last from six months to a year. That stage is a reactive emotion over which you might not have a lot of control. You just have to hang on, fasten your seat belt and know what is happening to you.

For the first few weeks he rang me every day. Sometimes he just wanted to say that he loved me, but mostly it was to blame our break-up on some drinking problem he insisted I had. I had no drinking problem. He just wanted to avoid facing the fact that our marriage was over — that it had died.

The middle stage is ANGER/GUILT/DEPRESSION. You can make this one last for the rest of your life if you want to. This is the bit you can more or less get under control, although you won't be able to avoid it. The pace of your recovery here is really your own. No one else can speed it up for you, but you should get firmly in your mind when you are in this phase the simple truth that there has to be more to your life than hanging on to a grief for a person who is no longer in it.

I made a small, but fierce bonfire out the back with some of his old underpants, socks and magazines he'd left behind and put a photo of us on the top. There were tears pouring down my face watching us burn, but it wasn't tight crying — it was a real letting go.

The final stage is ACCEPTANCE/UNDERSTANDING. Now you can face your former love and feel **in** not **under** control.

At first I hated being in our bed. It really seemed to underline what I had lost. It wasn't a sex thing. Not too much anyway because I had lovers pretty early on. It was just being alone in a place I wasn't used to being alone in. I used to stuff pillows down her side and I seemed to sleep better like that. Then one morning I woke early and couldn't get back to sleep. I didn't feel tired and I thought 'Damn. I'd really like to make some tea, read a book and open the curtains to watch the dawn sky through the window'. And then suddenly I realised I could do exactly that and anything else I wanted to do. I didn't have to defer to or be careful about or disturb anybody else. I had found out that you can be alone and enjoy it without being lonely. Sometimes I'm still lonely, of course, and in bed too, but that's all right, it isn't all the time like it was at the start.

There is probably no emotion more overwhelming than the feeling that your personal world is disintegrating, and contemplating a fearful future full of uncertainty. Denial of what is happening is a defence mechanism to help you absorb the pain. You will rocket from belief to disbelief at a sometimes terrifying pace. Just hang on and understand that what is happening to you is a perfectly normal process of emotional adjustment. Your emotions are in shock. This can be the worst phase of your whole adjustment. The next stage might seem worse, but you are in the driving seat then and you at least have a chance to steer around the bumps and potholes.

This is not the time to hide in corners – as much as you will feel like slinking away out of the world's sight. This is a time when you need all the tender loving care and nurturing you can get. But do be careful to make those who love you feel that they are helping. Don't drown them in tears or bore them to death.

Eventually the periods of disbelief and numbness wear off. Losing this animal protection can be hard going. Reality will now start to assert itself and you will have to look it right in the eye.

It took me a long time to face the rejection. When you have loved someone so passionately and then for him to reject you and your child (our baby was only eight months old) without a real explanation, it's just so cruel. My periods went crazy – I seemed to be bleeding all the time. I lost an alarming amount of weight.

I had no tits, no bum and no husband.

At this stage the 'where did I go wrongs' and the 'what ifs' can start to dominate your thinking. Some of those questions are ones you might need to answer. You are going to find it hard to avoid them in any case. Just make sure that it is you who is grasping the question and not the question that is grasping you. Remember that questions are just one half of a whole – you will find this a very rough phase if you just keep on repeating the question like a turkey gobbling in your mind. If you haven't got an answer then flag the question on – there probably isn't an answer anyway.

Friends and family who have supported you through the initial break-up will start to get on with their own lives. You may resent this. Don't. You are still going to need all the love and support you can get and their drifting away from your problem could be a positive sign that they know you are starting on another phase in your recovery.

About this time the loss of love might be joined by a feeling of less obvious losses. Loss of confidence, loss of family, fertility, hair, teeth, loss of direction and identity. Recognise that this is about the most stressful time in your life and be vigilant about the stress you are loading on yourself.

Stress can become a major health hazard. It can manifest itself in all sorts of frightening reactions. Psychological pain tends to accentuate your weakest points. If you tend to cry you will turn into a weeper. If you drink and smoke you will accelerate consumption. If you are quick-tempered (and sometimes even if you are not) your outbursts of rage may be alarming to those close to you. These are stress warning signs you should heed.

Sleeping patterns often go haywire. Any medical condition, both supposed and real may loom large as a health problem. Your mental stress will be causing your body to perform all kinds of unpleasant tricks on its wearer. Digestive and bowel upsets may convince you that cancer has struck and an erratic heartbeat might spell heart attack.

Do not ignore these signs either. Seeking help for an imagined illness may be a quick path to reassurance. In your thrall of panic about the future almost any disease you care to imagine can be made to fit your stress symptoms.

Two months after leaving the family home I was getting terrible, tense feelings – pains in my chest and a pounding heart. Physical symptoms that I could not control. They didn't seem related to specific things going on in my life. I went to see my doctor and told him about it. When he finished questioning me about my lifestyle and what had been happening to me he said he could fill me up with tranquillisers, but that wouldn't help me much. One small thing I could do was to cut down on coffee and alcohol. I should go away and come back in two months if my condition hadn't improved. Of course it did.

Focussing on any pain except the real one is a common reaction. But now is the time to face up to the fact that you **have** been rejected. You can't go back and change the past and there is no point in trying to assign blame or detect some cause. It is a good idea right now to write down somewhere your own version of this notion: EVERY CRISIS IS AN OPPORTUNITY and figure what you want to win out of this one.

The alternatives to facing reality now can be pretty hazardous. This is a time when you will be at real risk of embarking on some pretty destructive behaviour. Try doing some positive things – even if some of them might seem a bit bizarre.

Every time I went out and tried to get back to a normal social life I'd end up thinking about him and weeping. It was like a huge lump in my chest. A friend told me to wear a rubber band around my wrist and twang it every time I thought of him. It hurt, but it worked, and it even made me laugh.

The best medicine for me was laughter – better than any pills or vitamins. I had been taking things so seriously for so long I forgot about fun. A friend came round with a hired video and made me sit down and watch *The Man with Two Brains*. I laughed so much. It's bloody marvellous what a good laugh can do.

It is vitally important to look after yourself. Now is the time to be careful about diet, keep reasonably fit and get enough of the right kind of sleep. The fitter and stronger you are the quicker you will recover from the stress-induced physical and mental exhaustion of separation.

In the SHOCK/DENIAL phase your doctor might be able to prescribe some drug that will give you temporary relief from insomnia. Most doctors will warn you about the hazards of these and you should treat sleeping pills and sedatives with caution. There is no chemical answer to emotional problems, but with advice and care some mild drugs can help you to get the rest you need to cope.

In the ANGER/GUILT/DEPRESSION stage you may suffer more prolonged anxieties and your doctor might prescribe some minor tranquillisers. Treat these with even more caution. They can be dramatic mood improvers, but again they will do nothing to take away the cause of the anxiety. You will still have to face this when the drug wears off so it might be better to face it right away.

Many people find it extremely hard to get off drugs and a vulnerable few end up with an addiction.

It just became too simple to take a couple of those pale blue pills and float off and away each night. The few times I tried to do without them was just too hard and didn't seem worth the effort. Then when I finally got some real help, some counselling that really got to the root of my problem I knew that I was going to get better emotionally, but I was stuck with those damn pills. It took me nearly a year to wean myself away from them – long after the grief that I used them to dull had gone.

Before you go to your doctor, think about what a GP's role actually is. Most are too busy or lack the counselling skills to help you come to terms with emotional conflicts. A good GP will refer you to agencies which can help. A GP's role is mainly to treat symptoms, and the most cost-effective way to do that is with drugs.

At first, when there is something of a shady glamour about a broken heart, it might seem acceptable – like in the movies – to hit the booze or do drugs. Any glamour soon wears thin and the problem you end up with may be far worse and far more destructive than its cause.

Now is the time to remind yourself that you are not going to die of a broken heart. You will recover. Just get on with the process and don't try to bomb it away with drink or drugs. Masking the symptoms can prolong them.

Although less obvious a problem it is a good idea right now to be careful about your coffee intake. Coffee is a powerful stimulant, but when your adrenal glands are working overtime through stress, and if you have lost body weight, even seemingly normal amounts of coffee can have bizarre and frightening results.

Caffeine is thought to be a possible trigger in panic attacks – a terrifying, short spell of extreme fear with heart palpitations, dizziness, trembling, breathlessness and nausea. Prolonged stress can set off such an attack.

I drank coffee all day at work and didn't bother with cooking. The kids lived on hamburgers and Chinese takeaways. I didn't tell any of my friends what was really happening. I couldn't sleep and I was hitting the bottle and taking moggies, but I was managing okay at work – just. Then one night waiting at the station for my train I found I couldn't move. I could hardly breathe and my heart was going so fast I thought I was dying. I remember thinking – this is it. It was terrifying and I felt so helpless.

If you need to find solace in bottles or pills give the chemist and the off-licence a miss and try a health shop instead. Decaffeinated coffee, herb teas and various herbs and vitamins are kinder to an already overstretched nervous system. Orthodox medicine might argue that vitamins and herbs will do you no good, but they will certainly do you no harm. It is time to be kind to yourself.

Even though you are feeling hurt and angry you will also be feeling very alive. Your emotions, like nature, abhor a vacuum and the holes in your life are going to fill up again. The time it will take though, can be exhausting and turbulent so be aware of what your mind is doing to your body and give your body enough tender loving care to compensate.

I found it impossible to express my guilt and anger. It was just a part of my upbringing to suppress such things. Also I had left the marriage and forced the sale of our house. My husband had more to feel angry about. But in spite of all the positive feelings I had about being on my own, I was awash with guilt and angry at being so guilty. I used to go to the beach and walk thigh deep through the water along the beach. I felt like Sisyphus pushing his rock endlessly uphill. But it was a good physical way of exhausting my guilt. I got pretty fit too. Everyone thought I was training for the iron woman event.

Jealousy and a desire for revenge run deep in the human psyche. They are emotions that socially we are sensibly encouraged to suppress and they can also be a potent source of stress. You will need to acknowledge the reality and power of these parts of your nature and find ways of safely expressing them.

I felt so shitty and hated myself so much I didn't care what I did. I really packed up. I couldn't bear the thought of him still living in the same city in a sparkly new flat with a sparkly new woman when I was in our old place with our old chipped cups and a worn out me. What do you do about jealousy? It tore me to shreds and I felt ashamed of my feelings, but that didn't make them any less real.

Anger must be allowed to break out. Turning it inwards is a sure way to depression or even to thoughts of suicide.

Suicidal thoughts are a natural symptom of pain and rage that have been turned against yourself. Keep that idea in a place in your mind where you can find it easily in an emergency and use it to turn your pain and rage back out again.

Scream and shout if you want to. Indulge in some short sharp hate sessions on your own with you in control. You choose the time – don't let your rage into the driving seat.

There is nothing wrong with hate, if you are in charge. So pick a time and HATE the person you see as causing your pain: HATE the institution of marriage or the need for relationships that cause the pain: HATE society for the way it handles divorce and separation: HATE ANYTHING YOU WANT EXCEPT YOURSELF.

You don't have to be fair or reasonable. This is the part of the process when you put fairness and reasonableness firmly to one side. This is no time to behave well.

Bash pillows, howl, smash a plate or two (put your treasures away though).

Just keep in mind that, while expressing your anger is a good thing, out of control, unbridled anger is not good. The flow of adrenalin can make you feel as sick as the proverbial cat.

It's the end of a relationship – not the end of you.

After the separation she was full of a lot of anger and rage towards me. She couldn't hold it back. It just spilled out into many of our dealings with each other. She said that the physical separation had unleashed a lot of pain and rage that had been suppressed as long as we were still living together and trying to make a go of it. I couldn't cope with a lot of this anger, it made day-to-day communication over the kids a very painful process. I simply wasn't strong enough myself to take it all at that stage. Then one night about two months later we spent a long agonising evening telling each other quietly, but with a quite brutal honesty, what was happening to ourselves, including the involvement of other people. It was tearful and painful and almost unbearable for us both, but it really cleared the air and enabled us to recognise the other's position. Months later I find myself going back to that evening constantly.

Revenge, someone once said, is a sweeter dish if taken cold. In fact, it is a dish best not taken at all, but you may feel revengeful and it is not a bad idea to fantasise as a means of earthing some pretty dangerous stuff. Be outrageous if you want – the more outrageous and unreal your plots, the more chance you have of tipping feelings of revenge over the brink from a danger to yourself or your departed partner into some playful piece of mental surrealism.

This is a time, particularly for men in pain and anger, to monitor your revengeful feelings carefully and take advice immediately if they seem to be moving from fantasy towards reality. You are hurting. You have been rejected. None of this is a licence for you to hurt someone else, to make them fearful, to threaten or to bully.

At first I thought about him all the time and about the revenge I could wreak. I imagined fleet-footed raids – painting slogans on his new car, racing through his new woman's flat and chopping up her shoes. I didn't want to harm him – just all the things he'd got now without me. Those feelings lasted quite a while and I didn't suppress them.

I used to invent belittling names for her and her new man and make cruel jokes about them to my friends. When it rained one night at a dinner party, for instance, I told my hosts that this was exactly the kind of night I thought of her – and hoped she'd left her windows open. The odd thing was that as these jokes got wittier (and some of them were pretty good), even if the people I told them to didn't approve, they certainly got a laugh or two and I found less need to tell them.

I used to lie in bed with a bottle of gin and imagine fantastic revenges to relieve my rage. I imagined slipping into his room at night and cutting off his hair. I cackled at the thought of the look on his face when a hearse arrived at his door – sent by me. I thought dipping his dick in indelible green ink would be a neat trick.

No-one else can do your suffering for you, but you do need friends. It is a good first step to let your friends and relatives know about your situation. The ones who offer help will most probably be the ones who are best able to give it. Avoid casting your friends and family as bit players in your own real life drama and especially avoid forcing them to take sides. It's your separation, not theirs.

The heart and the head take quite different paths when something terrible happens like a lover leaves you. The head tends to scrabble along narrow dark paths in the brain, returning to the same point over and over again, like a rat in a cage. The heart rampages off on a roaring tumultuous rollercoaster ride, looping the loop, descending and soaring like a mad bird. I used to ring radio talk back shows at night. They put me on to Lifeline, who put me on to a wonderful counsellor who helped me stop wallowing.

In most cities, and in some smaller centres as well, professional help is available at the end of a telephone 24 hours a day. Sometimes an impartial ear is better than a close friend. There is usually a list of welfare organisations at the end of the Yellow Pages section of your telephone book.

Although it is you who has to make the journey through the whole process of grief, the caring help of professional counsellors or friends will make the journey seem less frightening and a lot easier to beat. Don't hide from help. Some help can really shorten the process if you let it.

At the other end of your grief, rage, anger and guilt is another life. It won't be the same, but it will be an adventure. Remember, even though you didn't choose it, you have been given a second shot at a whole lot of things – things that you can do and make better the second time around.

We'd had a row that night and she'd stormed out. Then she rang and said she didn't want to be hassled, but she was coming to get some things and she was leaving. I didn't hassle her. I wanted to plead with her, beg her to stay, but the words just wouldn't come. She packed a bag and went. I didn't know what to do. Eighteen years down the drain, just like that. I just didn't know what to do. I knew I wanted sympathy though and I rang a friend. A woman. We were very close. We had been lovers once. I said 'She's gone. Left me. What am I going to do?' and my friend said 'Well what do you expect to do but get on with your life.' I thought that was a bit harsh. I still think so. I know now, though, that it was the best advice I got for a long time.

CHAPTER THREE

Going

I didn't feel guilty about leaving. I hate making decisions. It took me eight years to decide to go. For eight years I knew it was wrong but I still believed I could make it work. For two of those eight years I knew I couldn't fix it but still I couldn't leave.

I left my first wife with no regrets and no remorse. We'd outgrown each other . . . or I'd outgrown her. Seventeen years later my second wife left me and the pain was like a knife in my brain. Part of this was understanding at last how my first wife had felt and what she must have suffered then and feeling the guilt of not having tried to make things work with her.

. . . .

Even if society is not good at coping with the traumas of separation it is at least more likely to sympathise with the grief of the person who has been left, than recognise the pain and problems of those who have chosen to leave. Many of these problems stem from exactly the same cause: social attitudes to marriage and other committed relationships, and judgements about 'failure', grief for lost love, fears about being alone, guilt. Some of the causes are different. The process, however, is very much the same.

Until death us do part is a very long time. Some relationships last the distance, many do not. What they all have in common, though, is, is growth and change. Nothing in our lives remains exactly the same – our lives would be very sterile and boring if they did. One of the expectations of youth is that life becomes more certain, stable and predictable with age. Happily that is not the case, although many people who are made anxious by change, resent and resist the fact that life goes on being challenging and demanding.

Our relationships are also subject to this dynamic. When they are working we adjust to the changes, consciously or unconsciously, in ourselves and in our partner. In strongly defined and consciously supportive relationships, growth and change in the partners is often welcomed and encouraged.

When relationships go wrong it is usually because those adjustments are not being made or the changes are not being recognised as they happen. Sometimes the changes seen by one partner in the other are felt as threatening that partner's security. Or in relationships in which one partner dominates, change is read as a challenge to that balance of control. The response is often one very similar to jealousy.

As I became more successful in my career I found I had to live a more public kind of life. My wife was very sociable and gregarious with our friends, but on formal or business social occasions she would become stand-offish or sarcastic and I found it easier not to include her. Soon we were living two quite different lives and although I still loved her I couldn't take the strain of it any more. It seemed so unfair that she couldn't support what was, after all, giving us a very good life . . . it was just as if she was jealous of me.

When the children left home I found the days really seemed to drag, so I started going to pottery classes at the local community centre. I got quite good at it and set up a pottery wheel in the garage. At first he was very supportive, but then he seemed to see it as some kind of a threat and resented the energy I put into it. If I was still working when he came home or if I wanted to pot on the weekends, he would make jokes about mud pies and things. He seemed to resent that I had something in my life other than him and our relationship, although I still ran our home and life with as much energy as before.

Often these kinds of responses are simply growing pains in changing relationships. Sometimes they are more than that and, as symptoms of far deeper problems, might easily become going pains. In any relationship it is always better to confront problems as soon as they become obvious. If difficulties that stem from growth and change are not worked through then the challenges they present are likely to become more and more confrontational and the demands of the threatened partner will escalate.

In the beginning he welcomed the new friends I was making through the part-time job I had started. He was always charming when they visited or if they rang. But then he began to get paranoid about them – they were all women. I think I might have understood his reaction if they were men friends – and accused me of all sorts of things, and them of plotting against our relationship. Eventually he said it was him or my job. I gave up the job. It was too much of a hassle not to, but I became very bitter about it and that was the beginning of the end.

I began to see her less as my partner and more like some difficult child who had to be pandered to. I certainly couldn't reason with her it seemed. Any new thing or suggestion would bring on a fit of sulking. Being annoyed with her became a habit.

Resentment in a relationship is something like a worm in an apple. Things might seem perfectly all right on the surface, but the nagging doubts and criticism are eating away at the substance. Quite trivial things begin to become a focus for completely unrelated anger and frustration.

The way he cleaned his teeth used to drive me crazy. He'd let the toothpaste run out of his mouth and drip down his arm and off the end of his elbow into the basin. It got so that I couldn't bear to be in the bathroom with him.

When we were first together I used to love the full on way she could enjoy herself. Then I found myself, when we were at a dinner party for instance, making silent cackling noises whenever she laughed and imagining sarcastic put-downs to her jokes. I thought I was going crazy and on the way home she couldn't understand why I was so subdued. The truth was I had worked myself up into an irrational rage and couldn't bear to speak to her.

We'd be out to dinner and I'd hear him start to tell a story I'd heard a million times before and I'd think: 'Oh, Jesus, here we go again'. He set my teeth on edge. Sometimes he made me so angry I couldn't even bear to look at his face.

Once this process has begun it is very difficult to reverse. Along with feelings of resentment, the partner falling out of love will almost certainly begin to feel trapped – another accelerant to add to the final flashpoint. The good and positive things about the relationship will now be buried in an increasing pile of emotional debris.

As difficult as it might seem to achieve, now is the time to stand back from all the confusion and ask some serious questions. How much are you doing to save or end the relationship? Are the things you resent, the familiar behaviours that set your teeth on edge, really the problem? If they are not, then what is? Are you really trapped, or is that an illusion caused by frustration or by fears about alternatives?

As a first step you could try talking the situation through with your partner. Let them know that you are feeling annoyed or frustrated, but try to minimise any cause for confrontation. Distance yourself from your anger or irritation and don't try to apportion blame or be judgmental, even if that means taking an approach that might seem to make you the cause of the problems.

You can be sure that your feelings have not gone completely unnoticed. If they have, then this effort will certainly not achieve much for the relationship. It is worth making, however, for your own feelings and as part of the process of letting go.

Your partner might also be feeling angry or frustrated about you. They may also be feeling hurt or helpless. It is useful to put aside any feelings you have about the problems being mutual, or your partner's fault alone, or that both are contributing to the breakdown and therefore both should take the initiative.

I precipitated the separation, but then I felt like the one who was left. It wasn't working and there was no acceptance that he had any part to play in this . . . he thought it was all my fault.

My needs weren't being met. In the beginning they were, but I changed and she couldn't. My anger and frustration in the marriage wasn't her fault. We simply couldn't be real. She was not into feelings at all.

Blaming is a common, almost instinctive, defence mechanism. In a relationship that is breaking down, however, it does not achieve much that is positive. It will certainly have the negative effect of concealing solutions and real causes, and in this situation that is the last thing you will need. Ideally this is the time for some very considered thought – a difficult trick to pull off in the midst of an emotional storm.

You are likely to be the one most acutely aware that something is amiss in the relationship. You will almost certainly have wondered if the problem is terminal. Your partner will probably not see things as clearly.

However heated the relationship has become, your decision to leave it is best not made in haste. It may be one of the most important choices you have had to make and you must think it through carefully and, if you can, coolly. Of course, some relationships can just be walked away from and in others it may be easier, economically and emotionally, for one of the partners to leave rather than the other. Whatever your situation, anticipating problems and difficulties is a major step towards coping with them or solving them.

It may be difficult, but the more you consider the situation of the person you are leaving, the easier you might find the aftermath. At the end of any long term relationship there are some quite practical decisions to make. Problems of property and children are major ones which are covered in later chapters. Such problems are better solved without the background of bitterness, anger or destructive emotions like revenge. This may mean that your patience might have to be called upon in waiting to resolve things that you may have wished to get on to more quickly than your ex.

I was absolutely devastated when he left, but I could hardly bear the pain of it all when I realised he had been planning this for over a year – he had bought another property, valued the house and everything we owned. It seemed so damned heartless that I was determined to do everything I could to make things bloody difficult for him, and with the help of my lawyer I did.

It will help if you think about the support systems you might need, family and friends for instance, where you might stay, what economic problems you will have to face. It is also important to know that, whatever your feelings of freedom and release, there will inevitably be some emotional adjustments to make. You may even experience the turmoil covered in the second chapter of this book.

The problems ahead may seem daunting, but you will need to face them and you should not use them as an excuse to stay in a situation that has become impossible. The longer you put off the inevitable, the more difficult some of those challenges might become.

Surprisingly, no matter how much the partner who makes the break has endured, planned or thought things through, the end of a relationship often comes as a bolt from the blue to the other partner. They may be completely unprepared for the split. You may have come to the end of your tether. You may be angry or even vindictive, but the easier you can make the break the better and the more productive it will be for both of you, not just for the one left behind.

One night I overheard her criticise me to one of her friends. Things had been wrong in our relationship for a long time, we'd become just two people living in the same house really, but I hadn't got to the point of deciding to go. I'd thought, 'This doesn't have much future, I wonder how long we can go on like this?' but I'd always been loyal and had never criticised her to anyone. I just saw red and said to her, 'We're not working out, I think we might as well split'. I think she was terribly surprised, but it was over for me, there was no going back.

Steve was moody and bad tempered a lot. I never knew where I was with him – sometimes he could be wonderful, at other times an absolute bastard, critical and rejecting, and it didn't seem to depend on anything I did. All my confidence went. I knew I shouldn't put up with his moods, and sometimes knew quite clearly I should leave him, but I was powerless to move. Then I went for a holiday to stay with friends I'd known before I ever met Steve. They treated me like the person I used to be – confident and in control of my life. I realised then how much I had changed and what a worm I had become. It shocked me so much I rang Steve and broke it off.

Women who leave a relationship have often worked through much of the process before they actually make the final break. Men are more likely to leave on impulse and sometimes go along with the break out of a kind of bravado.

I'd had it up to here! We'd been arguing for days – I can't even remember now what it was about – and finally I said, 'I want you to know that I really hate you and as soon as the kids leave home I'm going too'. He said, 'Well, if that's how you feel, why don't you go now?' and he walked into the room where the the kids were watching TV and said 'Your mother and I are getting a divorce'.

However the break happens, by considered choice or as the

sudden and inevitable end to an intolerable situation, it is still likely to stimulate emotional problems and adjustments. Even if you have chosen to leave a relationship that has been dead for years and even if leaving is an enormous relief, you may still have to cope with a sense of having failed at something you should have made work. You may also experience a great deal of guilt about the pain you might have caused.

I had the most appalling attacks of guilt after I left, particularly when I saw that he was managing okay and putting his life back together. All the unkind things I had ever done to him, all the criticisms and complaints came flooding back. Intellectually I knew the break-up wasn't all my fault, I knew we were not really suited and that even if we tried again it would just fall apart, but emotionally my body refused to believe it.

I left my wife for someone else. I didn't feel bad at the time, but she was devastated. For me, the thought of the new woman was exciting and I'd pretty much convinced myself that it was my ex's fault that our relationship had run aground. But as the weeks went by, the new relationship ran into problems. They were the same problems the old had come to grief on, and I couldn't avoid the fact that they were my fault. I started thinking about my wife all the time – she was never out of my head. I didn't want to go back, but I felt I had desperately wronged her, I hadn't really tried in the relationship at all. It was even worse to think that I couldn't seem to get it right in a new relationship either.

There is really no way of avoiding feelings like these. It is best to confront them and to come to terms with the real cause of your guilty feelings. It helps to keep in mind that your situation is not unique. Others have been there and done that, are there and doing that! Yes, your relationship has come unstuck, but that does not mean you are a failure or that successful relationships are beyond you.

When I left I became obsessed about the relationship. All I did was talk about it to my friends, it was on my mind all the time – things I could have done to make it work, reasons why it wouldn't have. I couldn't leave the relationship alone, it was so unhealthy.

Five years later I worry that I'll always be the person who can't accept things, that there is something wrong with me, that I'll be alone all my life.

Providing it does not become an obsession and that you genuinely search for answers, questioning the reasons for the failed relationship is a reasonably healthy thing to do. You may have done things differently. You may have been a major cause of the problems in the relationship. Understanding that is one of the best ways of knowing what to avoid the next time around.

That is if you decide that there will be a next time. Being single is a rich and positive lifestyle too and for some it can be the richest and most positive choice.

Working through these feelings of guilt and failure is something you must do if you want to avoid carrying them into another relationship. Even if you have come to terms with your own attitudes and behaviours, which you know can cause problems, just the fact that you are carrying a burden of guilt about the past can cripple or destroy a new relationship.

I tried so hard to make it work. I really loved him, but I couldn't get past the fact that he put his old family first. He would break dates because something came up with his children. Or he would be late because his ex-wife needed some problem solved or something fixed round the house. He'd left the marriage, but they'd kept him on as a handyman or something and I began to despise him for it. I did admire him at first, but then it just seemed to be more wimpish than noble. If I'd wanted to have an affair, I would have picked a man who was really married.

Feelings of grief can easily get mixed up with feelings of failure. Even if the relationship was an absolute disaster it almost certainly did not start out that way. Grieving for lost love or lost opportunity should be resolved. In many ways this is one thing that those who are left and those who leave have in common. The circumstances are different, the causes are different, but the grief is likely to be much the same for both.

One day I realised I didn't admire him any more, not anything about him – the magic had totally gone. I actually cried for what we had lost. Who was the balding, paunchy, irascible man who had haemorrhoids and made grunting noises in his sleep? Where was my Peter Pan?

I left my husband when I was 32. In the beginning I had no guilts and no regrets, the world was my oyster – I was free. After six months I was finding it difficult to cope on my own with the children, with the strain of being solely responsible for their welfare, the income and looking after the home. Then the guilt and regret set in and the desire to try again surfaced.

The hardest thing for me when I left my wife was the loss of multiple roles. My children both went overseas at the time we split up so I was no longer a husband, a father nor the breadwinner. I realised that I didn't even have any friends who weren't hers, so I wasn't even a friend. I felt totally bereft.

One of the dangers about feelings like these is that they can so easily lead to you sending quite false signals to the person you have left. Compassion and caring is fine, but there is nothing quite so cruel as false hope. So, whatever you are feeling, whatever support and comfort you are searching for, be scrupulous about protecting the other person from your temporary emotions. They are temporary. They will pass but your decision to end the relationship is permanent.

Life on your own may be challenging and difficult. You might yearn for the old securities. When that happens it is not a bad idea to sit down and force yourself to think of the reasons why you left. You have to constantly define that decision as a positive choice and a new opportunity.

He said, 'You can't expect me to look after you. You'd better start paying some board.' I'd given up four children, a wonderful home and a loving husband for a huge con trick. I felt cheated. I saw myself as inferior and cheap and not part of the world today.

When I first left I didn't feel too bad, but when she got into another relationship and I was still into the one night stands, I crumbled. I suppose you'd say that when she was no longer waiting in the wings that the guilt and the remorse and the sense of aloneness hit.

The old life is over. You made that choice. It is a waste of energy and opportunity to use illusions about the past to protect you from confronting the new. Remind yourself again why and how you made the choice. Think of what your life might still be like if you hadn't. No matter how you are feeling right now, or how difficult starting again might seem, there is nothing more sterile or lonely than staying in a dead relationship.

Being loved and loving are creative, generative states. Even if you are not 'in love', life is a sorry business without enthusiasm, growth, challenge and change. None of these things have a chance when you are conditioned only by a sense of obligation, habit, an enervating dependence, or fear of the new.

Of course, your choices are affected by other people. But in the end your contribution to them is more likely to be enhanced if you are living life as a whole, self-determined and self-reliant person.

One day I realised: 'I am destroying me'. I'd sat around for a year feeling guilty and trying to see if there was any basis for a reconciliation and wanting things to be different than they were. From that day I've felt totally liberated — it's finished. I'm free. I've worked through it.

I stayed in the marriage for years and years after it was dead, and coping after I left was very difficult. I wish I'd left earlier, I would have had all that energy, I could have done so much more with my life.

I didn't leave because I didn't love him. I left because it was too painful to stay.

I was over the moon to be out of it, but then the grieving hit me. I couldn't understand why. I had what I wanted, I was free, but I felt more miserable than I'd ever been and I realised you just can't cut something like that out of your life without feeling something and making some adjustments. Once I'd come to terms with that I began to snap out of the misery and get on with things.

CHAPTER FOUR

Sorting Things Out

I wish we'd sorted things out a lot more before he went. He slammed out saying he didn't want anything more to do with us and that he didn't want anything. But a few months later he started coming round and hassling me about the things he wanted that were 'his'. The kids and I were starting to do okay — beginning to recover and get on line again, but having to face him and niggle over little things put me in a real tizz. If only we had sorted things out at the time.

At first I'd go through wildly swinging feelings about her. One day I'd want her to remain my best friend while the next day I'd feel so raw and hurt that I couldn't bear to speak to her to make arrangements about the kids. I'd be angry and resentful. Then I read a book which urged separated couples to treat their relationship in a businesslike manner. In business it's not important whether you like or dislike the other person, it said — you simply deal efficiently with the matter in hand then go your separate ways. In fact you deliberately try to get the negative emotions out of the transaction. I thought that was very wise.

In fact I mentioned it to her and we decided to use it as a basis for our dealings with each other.

. . . .

Rational, intelligent adults take some pride in sorting out their problems in rational and intelligent ways. In the transactions that immediately follow a separation it is quite amazing how irrational and stupid you might find you or your ex-partner can be. Something as trivial as the ownership of a favourite pot plant can turn you into a raging monster.

I had promised myself that when the time came for her to take the things she wanted and needed from the house, I would be cool and 'civilized' about it. In the event I didn't have the opportunity to be either. I came home from work just as two removal men were loading the last of the large pot plants from the garden into their van. I demanded they put it back immediately, threatened to call the police and charge them with theft if they didn't – made a real fool of myself. I wanted to be adult about the whole thing, but she hadn't even consulted me – just came when I was out and helped herself – so much for being 'civilised'.

Counselling and conciliation through neutral third parties, like your solicitor or the In-Court Services, may take the friction out of sorting out the huge problems and decisions necessary for the final parting. But the stress involved in sorting out the small things and having to deal, face to face, with the person you have finally parted from can be enormous.

Learning how to communicate without too much pain, keeping cool under heavy fire and curbing your own desires to score cheap points should become a priority. A critical first step is to have worked out clearly in your own mind the essential purpose of the encounter – what result you want from the transaction – before you enter it.

It is a good idea to make a list. Write down what it is you want and stick to that agenda for the meeting. Don't allow your own feelings, or those of your ex, to sidetrack you. It is easy enough to be civilised and reasonable in the professional atmosphere of the court or solicitor's office, but on home turf behaviour can all too easily become distinctly primitive.

After the initial storms of rage and grief have settled, bitterness and outrage often emerge. Resentment can easily swamp reason – all the more so when the transactions between yourself and your partner have a material edge to them. Few separations are clear cut enough to deal with all the material ramifications at the beginning. Even those who knew separation was imminent can find settling down immediately to the cold-blooded divvying-up of the family property a little too heartless.

Once the physical moving away of one partner has occurred – whether you are dancing for joy or weeping and wailing – a stage has been passed which makes it harder to decide on anything about the old life.

You may disappear behind rose-tinted lenses, remembering only the good times and agreeing to anything. Or you may be so ridden with guilt that you hesitate to claim anything for your future life. Or you may be so consumed with rage and set for revenge that nothing short of total ruin will seem good enough for your ex. You may even feel all three of these things in the same day!

I have never felt so close to murder. I hadn't time to go out and collect a lot of my stuff and the bitch had given all my carpentry tools to her bloody hippy brother — my father had given them to me and I treasured them. All my records had gone to a second-hand shop and I had to buy them back.

If you are the one moving out, take all your personal treasures with you. Leaving precious personal belongings behind give mixed messages that you may be undecided about the split, or want to hedge your bets. If you have decided to part, then making that absolutely clear and unambiguous is the kindest message you can give at the start.

Leaving your treasures behind can also make them hostage to the other partner's revenge. Understandably enough, in the absence of the person their material possessions can become a convenient object for rage.

Pack up your books, papers, tool, clothes, things you value and things you had from your life before marriage or the relationship. Leave a list of what you have taken and keep a copy for yourself in case of any disagreement later.

Most people when they leave the family home, leave the household goods behind. Where children are involved it is most usually the custodial parent who will stay and it is usually that parent who will have the most obvious claim on the household basics. Whoever leaves, though, will need at least the minimum of equipment to start out again – linen, blankets, a few kitchen utensils. If taking these causes fights, then leave them. It is easy enough to pick up cheap bedding and basic bits and pieces from bargain houses or second-hand shops. In case of genuine economic distress, a citizens' advice bureau can direct people in need to church and other agencies who provide cheap or free household basics.

Avoiding scenes about possessions reduces a lot of anguish and stress. You may feel deeply attached to the family pots and pans right now, but in a week or so you will probably find it hard to recall with any accuracy just what they were like.

The departing partner will, in most circumstances, have to accept that a reduced material standard of living is probably an inevitable price to pay for the separation. It might seem cold comfort at the time, but often material things can carry with them all kinds of emotional triggers and it is sometimes easier to start from scratch.

A year or so after we had split a new woman moved into my life and into my house. I thought I had such a neat lifestyle and environment that she would just be happy to be a new part of it – very naive of me that was, and insensitive – the material ghosts of the old relationship haunted her until eventually we split too. How stupid to hang on to bits and pieces of furniture when they cost me what might have been a very happy new marriage. Of course I wasn't hanging on to those things. Deep down I was hanging on to my old love and my new lover knew and resented that.

One school of thought says it is healthy to fight over material goods, that it shows you really valued what you are now breaking up. Most people, though, would agree that such squabbles are more likely just to emphasise mean and petty emotions – the fighting is not about possessions at all, but simply a prolonging of the personal battles.

In the early stages of a separation, most people's feelings are pretty raw and very close to the surface. Even if one partner is happy to be free of the marriage or relationship, their impatience to put it behind them and get on with their new life can make them intolerant of the other's hurt and anger.

Accept that the relationship is over. You have no obligations to it left. You can walk away from the anger and rage – you can refuse to play any games of taunts and recriminations. Often challenges from your ex about being a bitch, a wimp or a coward and exhortations to face up to the issues can be translated as 'stay here and be punished'. You don't have to – so don't.

You are not being weak by refusing a fight. You certainly will not help yourself or the other person by pouring oil on the flames. In the midst of a blazing row you are certainly not going to achieve any real agreement about the things the encounter was supposed to resolve. Walk away and negotiate another day.

When you meet rage, try and find a reason other than yourself for it – your ex may be having lover trouble or the car may be playing up. See yourself as the recipient of the rage and not necessarily its cause.

In some situations you can defuse the anger and advance a little towards a new relationship. Some people find that going along with the accusations hurled at them – 'Yes. I am a wimp',

'Of course I'm useless' and so on – can turn a livid scene into something both participants will find funny. Exaggerating the accusations and ending up with such ridiculous admissions can create a situation where laughter is the only way out. But treat such episodes with caution. You should know from your relationship where the tolerance levels are and attempts at defusing a potent row with humour can also be provocation.

My wife was in a white rage. The kids were crying in their bedroom and she was in full flight. She said she was going to kill me and reached into the kitchen drawer for a knife. I was shouting. We were both totally out of control. She grabbed something and when she held it up ready to attack, we saw she had a funny old spatula in her hand. There was one of those thundering seconds of silence before we both exploded with laughter. But that experience shook us to our roots. We planned our meetings very carefully after that – always with a friend present.

If your meetings are likely to get out of hand, using an intermediary is the best way of avoiding out-of-control behaviour. Some anger is justifiable, even if the person to whom it is directed doesn't want to hear about it.

It is important to listen to what is being said. A close friend is often able to umpire a meeting and allow the aggrieved person to say what they feel without interruptions from the other.

Angry people do not make good decisions and commonsense should tell you that rage is not an ingredient of any reasonable compromise. The decisions you make now may not be about the big issues, but they may set a pattern which will show up later when you have to decide on the major things like matrimonial property, maintenance or children.

Trading insults, loud disavowels and meeting accusation with accusation is not going to take you anywhere. These behaviours are the quickest way to generate heat in an argument. Anger may prevent you from hearing something important.

Learn to apologise if you do explode.

If you find yourself repeating fight patterns you had when you were still together, just remember you are not together now, the relationship is different, so leave those old responses behind.

Leaving my husband, teenage kids and house took such a lot of courage I didn't have much left to face sorting things out afterwards. The kids wanted to stay in their own house. My concentration when I left was totally on getting going on my own and I couldn't think about going back and sorting out my stuff. It made it extremely hard for my ex. He couldn't bear seeing my old gumboots in the wash house or bits and pieces that were mine left around the house. He wanted a clean sweep too, but I didn't think about that or how I was delaying his recovery.

Separation can bring with it considerable economic problems. Even if one partner was in a non-earning supportive role in the relationship, the freedom that provided the other in terms of earning and work patterns most probably had a major influence on the family finances.

Time and planning – and planning with a clear head – can resolve some of these major problems. Neither of you should rush or be rushed into confronting them at the very outset of the bust-up. There may be some more immediate losses to resolve first.

Almost every relationship develops some instinctive support systems. Few couples do everything within the relationship. By choice or instinct or habit they have divided up the tasks and skills they need to function. Often these extend outside the relationship into social patterns which may have taken years to develop.

Becoming uncoupled can mean losing a network of friends and neighbours who have shared childcare, tool-borrowing, transport-pooling and a host of other things you simply took for granted. Losing these intangible things can be as traumatic as material losses.

Again, being aware of them is an essential first step to their replacement. Some of them you may not need, of course, but if you have been operating as part of a supporting network, the world can suddenly seem barren, cold and, perhaps, frightening when it is no longer there.

Often it is the woman who bears the brunt of this kind of loss. Men suffer it too, but the usual pattern is that men are less immediately dependent on it. But if the male suddenly becomes the custodial parent, he may not have actually realised how much community input went into parenting and feel hopeless as a result.

Meanness and rage might encourage you to keep this kind of practical knowledge to yourself, but it will greatly enhance your self-respect if you can put such feelings aside and make sure your ex gets as much help as you can give him or her in the necessary readjustment. Some of that help might be unwelcome. Your attempts to offer it might earn you a painful rebuff. But as a general rule of thumb there are greater benefits – mostly emotional but sometimes material – in helping than in not.

If your partner is not around to help, then make sure you know where to get what material or practical help you need. A Citizens' Advice Bureau will direct you to a whole structure of agencies for advice and help. So too will the DSS in case of material hardship or threats to the welfare of you or your children.

No-one can know what it feels like until it happens to you. My husband had been going off for months in his suit – I thought to work, but he had been made redundant and thought he could find another job without causing us worry. The further he got into this fantasy the more he covered up. He borrowed enormous amounts of money – men in suits can – then he disappeared. We were left with a letter from the bank about the mortgage. I had three children under ten, no income, and a house that was owned by the bank.

Not all situations are this extreme, but a great many separations bring immediate hardships, even if just for a short period of adjustment. Don't hesitate to seek official help if you feel that your family situation is threatened – if your home is at risk for instance.

You might never have given the notion of welfare benefits any real thought as something that would one day apply to you. If you suddenly have to confront it, then don't punish yourself or your children through some false pride. You have paid for those support systems through your taxes. When you need them yourself just keep in mind that you are simply claiming an insurance on which you have spent a lifetime paying the premiums.

The bureaucratic structure of state welfare systems can seem harsh, unfeeling and tedious. It is, if you don't bother to find out the rules first. Again check with a citizens' advice bureau. Before you apply make sure you know what benefits are available, what you are eligible for or entitled to, and how to apply without wasting some harassed clerk's time or straining your own already frayed nerves.

My parents wanted me to go and live with them while I got my life back together. But they weren't very well off. They lived in a neat house in a 'respectable' suburb and they were horrified at their darling daughter joining the solo mother set and being a 'dole bludger'. But I was only on the benefit for eight months while I found a place and did a refresher course so I could go back to teaching. Believe me, it was a nightmare time, but two years on I feel far more secure and in charge than I did in a shaky marriage. I appreciated keeping independent.

For a great many women – and perhaps a few men – becoming single may also mean going back to work. In some cases it may mean going to work for the very first time, or at least so long after previous work experience that it will seem like the first time.

In a difficult economic climate the need to go back to work can be an enormous source of stress. It is also a challenge to find new work skills or hone old ones. In a bad employment climate there are usually a great many work skills programmes offering. Check them out. A citizens' advice bureau or the Job Centre will know what is available in your area.

Enrolling in such programmes can have more than simply economic benefits. They offer a chance to meet new people. They are also one more step on the road to a new sense of self-respect. Often people embedded in a relationship have an increasingly narrow view of their own abilities, being challenged to develop new skills can be marvellously therapeutic, if a little daunting at first.

Sometimes the emotional trauma of becoming single and the sheer weight of practical problems and decisions can become just too much to cope with. Seek help as soon as you feel you are slipping under these pressures. Initially friends and relatives can be an excellent source of advice and support, but you may need more.

We'd got into the fatal situation of talking about problems and him giving me my maintenance money when he picked the kids up on Thursdays. I'd drone out the same old complaints and he'd defend in the same old aggressive way. It was like a traffic jam where no new ways of behaving could emerge. We both had power over each other to hurt and we weren't going to let it go — he could withhold money and I could withhold access. In the end I went to a course on anger and grief resolution which literally was like lifting the scales from my eyes. There are people out there with fantastic skills to help people who are hurting.

Five years ago, when we were having difficulties together, we'd gone to a woman at the marriage guidance service and found it very useful. She seemed very perceptive and rather clever. She helped us work through some problems. This time it is very different. We've gone back to this woman several times, but it's clear that we were getting nowhere. So now we've decided not to go back. We're separating and that's that. The counsellor has still been useful – not in bringing us back together – more in helping each of us get into our own feelings.

The problem with counselling is that when you really need it you may not know you do or will refuse to admit it. Listen carefully if people who are close to you talk about counselling. It will certainly do you no harm and it may unlock a lot of firmly closed doors and let a lot of light and air into a very gloomy state of mind.

The citizens' advice bureau or Law Centre can give you information about counselling services or courses. There is a whole range available but some of them may need to be treated with caution. There is no point, for instance, in plunging into some heavy rebirthing seminar, when the ordinary problems of everyday life are already generating trauma.

When you are emotionally vulnerable you can easily fall prey to the emotional dependency some fringe therapies offer. They work for some people, of course, but they may not relate to the specific needs or emotional storms of the newly separated.

I had drifted into a group of people who were like me – newly separated and hurting a lot. We gave each other a lot of support which really helped in the bad patches. It was as if we talked a language and understood experiences our other couple friends could not. One of the group took up with a self-realisation fad – one of those high pressure, quick talk, brainwashing therapy things. In no time at all she was like a frantic stranger. We could see the harm it was doing her and all the energy she was putting into a false high which, sooner or later, would give her a nasty fall into an even greater emptiness than the one she thought she was escaping.

Listen carefully to the experiences of friends who have had counselling. Some of them will want to sell you on their own enthusiasm, but at least they have been there and can give you some idea of what may help you. Your doctor may know of a good counsellor or, quite rarely, might offer counselling.

Church groups often run counselling services or courses, but again be a little cautious of those that are too fundamentalist. You will have enough guilt and sense of failing to cope with, without adding fire and brimstone to the mixture.

Pain and rejection will, naturally, bring out a yearning for tribalism in most of us. Be careful not to let this feeling propel you into some cranky cult or group that you would immediately reject if you were feeling better about yourself and the world.

The anger of separation can easily spill over into physical violence. Violent behaviour will solve nothing – you simply cannot punch or pummel or terrorise someone back into loving you. There are a number of men's support groups who provide counselling for potentially or actually violent men. Don't hesitate to contact them if you are fearful about the potential results of your anger or if you have an inclination to violence.

There are an enormous number of resources available to help the newly separated sort things out. Many of them are listed in the Yellow Pages of your telephone book.

After a lot of mucking about and self-destructive behaviour I finally took a friend's advice and got some counselling. I went to a psychotherapist – although she wasn't called that or I wouldn't have gone near her – and she gave me one session of something called transactional analysis. I was a mess. I simply froze and for half an hour or so I don't think I understood a word she said. Then it clicked. It was bloody marvellous. Like coming out of prison. For the first time since my wife dumped me I was able to stand back from myself and make some choices. I wanted to make another appointment, but she said 'Why? You're going to be okay' and I was. Of course, I slipped back every now and then, but I knew how to get going again, thanks to her.

CHAPTER FIVE

How Shall We Tell
the Children?

It was like those creepy old stories where naughty children are locked in dark cupboards for being bad. I felt like that – that I was being kept in the dark. Dad was never there and Mum was so preoccupied. She kept saying nothing was the matter, but I could see there was – she cried a lot and flared up at the slightest thing. I imagined terrible things. I thought it was my fault. I just about went mad. I thought if I ran away things might get better and Dad would come back.

Later that day, the day she left, she went and picked our son up from school and dropped him off at the gate. I heard the car and went out. It was the minute I had been really dreading. But my son just gave me a big grin and said 'I'm going to stay with the one that keeps the swimming pool'. I thought 'You callous little bugger' and then I thought 'Well he's got to cope too'. But when we got inside the gate, and his mother had driven off, he put his arms around me and burst into tears. I said 'We'll be all right' and I knew we would be and that he was going to stay with me. For a while anyway. Later he told me that he just wanted to say that it was his house, near his friends and his school and whatever

I and his mother had decided about ourselves that's were he wanted to be. For a while anyway. That seemed fair enough to me.

. . . .

No matter how careful and sensitive you have been, your children will have been getting some very loud signals from your disintegrating relationship. Even very young children will have picked up some of what has been going on – that Mummy and Daddy are having a rough time. If they haven't heard any fights they will certainly have felt the chilly or strained atmosphere.

But whether your break-up has been 'civil' or a red hot battleground, children need to know what is going on. They can cope with quite large amounts of truth – it is uncertainty and anxiety that may damage them. When their parents' relationship falls apart, nearly all children feel in some way that they are really to blame. These feelings of guilt and unease will only increase if they are constantly fobbed off with empty statements or ignored.

Your relationship may be over, but being a parent is not.

My daughters are teenagers and to begin with I found it very difficult to find things for us to do together. I mean you can't take them to the zoo as if they are six years old. And they're busy with their own lives and their own friends. I have them to my flat for meals, but I've found the best way for us to spend time together is to involve myself more in their activities. So I attend all their sports events, for example. I sometimes pick them up and drop them off somewhere, maybe just to a friend's place. I meet them after a movie and take them home. It's short contact sometimes, but it's real and ordinary and it means I'm taking some responsibility for them. It also means I have to spend more time at their mother's place than I'd like, which is often a bit tense because there is another man there now. But I'm committed to making this work. I'm not married any more, but I'm not going to stop being a parent.

Telling the children needs a great deal of care. It might seem just one more unbearable task piled onto all the other things you are feeling. But if you do sort the situation out for your children you may have taken a big step towards sorting things out for yourself. At the very least you will have one less thing to worry or feel guilty about and sometimes children can be wonderfully supportive.

One thing is certain, your relationship with your children is not going to be the same. It could even be better. It might require an entirely new investment of your emotional energy and you may need to learn some new parenting skills.

At first I tried not to cry in front of the children. I held on, bottling it up, shoulders almost under my ears sometimes. Then once when I did burst into tears they were so good — patted my back, cried too and hugged me. It was a tremendous release for us all. There are so many different things to cry for, but I'm sure now that it is much better to let go rather than be stoic. Children understand so much more than you think. I had cut off from them, but once it came out I got to know them so much better and they were a source of strength I hadn't realised before.

We had shared a lot of the domestic things in the marriage, but I suppose our roles were still pretty well defined along conventional lines. Suddenly I became a solo parent with almost total responsibility for a very demanding 13-year-old boy. Basking in the applause of friends for the occasional Saturday night culinary triumph is one thing, but turning on a sensible and attractive meal seven nights a week is something entirely different. I began to enjoy it and, after a while, so did he. We started to enjoy being together during that domestic routine and despite the inevitable father and son head banging we laid down the foundation of a genuine friendship, which even continued to flourish when a few years later, for very sensible reasons, he decided to go and live with his mother. He is a young man now and our relationship is much more than just that between father and son.

A major part of how children react to their parents' separation will depend on how the parents themselves cope. From all the stories told by separated parents, and the research of psychiatrists, family therapists and psychologists, the better you cope the better your children will come through the experience. This is equally true for both parents – the one who leaves and the one who stays. Of course the children will have some scars, however well you do, but the process of emotional growth leaves all children with some scars – whether their parents have separated or not.

Hanging on in a bad and destructive relationship is probably more likely to harm the children than a break-up.

Kids react to the fraught atmosphere in the house. They must lie in bed in the dark wondering what the hell is going on and wondering if they are to blame. My ex-husband had the traditional boys' schooling – mates but not friends, competition and conflict to achieve and win. He could never discuss anything – it turned into a debate. He never raised his voice, just dominated by clever and superficial language that reduced me to silent and impotent rage. We've been so much happier since he left. And so has he.

I felt I was a much better parent after we split. The kids' lives were definitely better away from the doom and decay of our marriage. I had taken all the initiative and though I'd feel guilty, but the relief was so great. The kids' social life rocketed when they felt they could bring their friends home. My wife moved out into a small flat and the kids visited her there, on her terms.

When parental behaviour seems odd and things are obviously changing in the family it is not reasonable to expect children to carry on as if everything were normal. They are deeply involved in the changes too. They are also committed, from a different viewpoint, to the relationship that is coming adrift. The children will feel the insecurity, but they have no way of controlling what is happening so if they react with odd or destructive behaviour they are only reflecting their fear of the unknown.

The whole pattern of your life is changing and so is theirs. You have quite a lot of choices that are not available to them. Your children may not recognise you as you enter the anxious zone of the about-to-separate parent. Nor may they particularly approve of the outward signals of a changed lifestyle or image you may decide to adopt.

My whole appearance changed. I cut off my long hair (that he liked) and dyed out the grey streaks (that he thought becoming). I started wearing lots of make-up (that he didn't like) and wearing jeans (that he hated). My two girls, aged 9 and 12 were amazed. Apparently it's very common to change your appearance when you separate and because they had accepted that they took the changes in their stride too – after they got over the first shock that is.

As soon as you can, tell your children exactly what is going on in a way that they will easily understand. How you actually tell your children is rarely how the experts say is the best way. There is a best way of doing it though and the closer you can get to that, the easier it will be to communicate with your children.

Ideally, both parents should tell the children together. All the details about contact, residence and holidays should have been worked out in advance. Unhappily, the ideal is usually not the real situation and both of you will probably still be at opposite poles when it is time to tell the children.

If the situation is likely to descend into a slanging match or a seething mess of violent emotions, then it is better for one parent to go it alone. You may find it easier to enlist the help of a close friend or relative the children know and trust to help explain things or answer questions they may not be able to ask you.

In the majority of separations it is the man who leaves the family home. In this situation it is usually the mother who is left to break the news to the children. The children may then hear their mother's story and may have to balance that later against a completely different version from their father.

Whatever else you do, avoid turning the children into a battleground. They have enough to cope with and to dump on them is inexcusable, no matter what you feel and how justified your anger at the other partner might seem. Conflicting or blame-throwing stories can divide loyalties and lead to long-term problems. In younger children, hearing the news in this way can even plant a deep-rooted fear of the absent parent, which can poison their relationship for the rest of their childhood.

Your relationship with your partner may have finished, but your children have still got, and are going to need, two parents. You are helping no-one by undermining their trust in their other parent. You may feel betrayed, but you have no reason to make the children feel the same way. Your wounds are going to heal. You may even find another partner who will provide an immensely better relationship than the one you are grieving for. Your children are not going to be able to replace a parent.

Worst of all is a silent parent. Fear of the unknown can be much more damaging to a child than knowing that their parents have split and that their life is going to change in a whole lot of ways – no matter how initially upsetting that may be.

I said I'm not going to tell them . . . you're the one who's leaving . . . you tell them. And he did, one at a time. There were lots of tears and wailing, but I think he handled it very well. He was loving and reassuring in a way that I couldn't have been. I wonder now if I was using telling them as a sort of spiteful message to him. In any case I wasn't up to telling them and my feelings then wouldn't have helped them at all.

My husband and I told the children together when my husband finally decided to leave. We'd read all the advice about how to do it properly and the best sort of words to use, but nothing can really prepare you for the horror of actually breaking the news. Our eldest son was 14 and he rushed from the room and cried all night buried in his bed. Our 12-year-old girl went all cool and said it suited her fine and she couldn't care less. The 5-year-old didn't really understand very much, but cried anyway. For me that night was really the guillotine end to my marriage, and with three such different reactions I didn't know which way to turn. But it was the only way really.

There are infinite variables in just what you have to tell the children. It will depend on their age range, how long the marriage has lasted, how it broke up – either a slow descent into indifference or a sudden, unexpected explosion – and how much disruption to the children's physical surroundings there may be. You don't, of course, have to blurt out all the bad news at once – just enough to cope with the immediate reality.

Whatever you have to tell the children, however, there are three basic points you should take a lot of care over.

● Tell the children the truth and be as honest as you can about the details. Obviously just how much detail you need to tell will depend on the range of the child's understanding

– a 5-year-old's need for detail will be a lot less than that of a 12-year-old, for instance.

● Make sure the children know that they are not to blame. This is about the most important personal message you can get across to your children. This is the first reassurance they are going to need.

● Make sure that your children understand that they still have two loving parents even if they are no longer going to live together.

Just how much you need to tell the children will depend on how much they have picked up already, as well as their capacity to understand. Some will only be able to cope with the bare minimum of facts to start with and will bit by bit ask for new information as they absorb the old. Others may want to spend a great deal of time going over points, asking and repeating questions and wanting as much information as possible.

Body language plays a big part in how children sense just what state of mind their parents are in. Try not to send them confusing signals – it will not help them much if you tell them everything is okay while you are strangling a handkerchief or tearing the heads off the flowers.

Let them know exactly how you feel. Explain that you are upset and that you may act a little strangely from time to time, but that it is not their fault. Make them feel that there are times they can cheer you up and perhaps times when you just might be too stitched up for hugs and kisses. Children know a lot more about emotions than we sometimes give them credit for. Children can also be frightened by adult emotions. If you know you are in for a few uncontrollable storms make sure there are friends or relatives near by who can provide the children with a secure haven.

My son could understand my grief and my sadness, but he couldn't cope with my rage. He could take on the fact that I was sad to lose his mother whom he also loved, but he was defensive and hurt when I said harsh or hateful things about her. Actually it did me no harm to get the verbalising of that, a bit under control.

There are some no-go areas you should keep in mind when you are telling the children. If you say Mummy and Daddy don't love each other any more a child can quite easily leap to the frightening conclusion that Mummy and Daddy could just as easily give up on loving them.

Keep it simple. Just say that Mummy and Daddy are going to live in separate places from now on, but that having two loving parents is not going to change.

Do no apologise. An apology is a confusing signal to a child when it is about something that is not going to be changed back or repaired. Do put the step you are taking in the most positive light. Emphasise that even if what you have decided to do is making you unhappy just then, in the not too distant future, everyone will really be better off.

Use the word 'we' when explaining the decision to the children so they don't take exception to one or other parent and feel they have to take sides. As hard as it might be just then, it will help your children if you adopt a united front as parents and that living apart is something you have both decided to do.

Do not resent the fact that your children are going to react, however well you have broken the news. Let them show their feelings.

My kids gave me a very hard time at first – quite vicious sometimes. They blamed me for breaking up the family – they did it to their father too. They could really wound.

All children want their parents to get back together. They will make that one of their favourite fantasies. More in your control is the fact that they want to see their parents in moods they recognise. Very young children might not grasp the facts of what is going on, but they are in tune with how things feel.

If their parents spend hours on the telephone, in intense conversations with friends or just gazing vacantly into the middle distance they can very easily conclude that Mum or Dad has gone AWOL and plunge into insecurity. This will set up a clingy 'am I to blame' response in the child. They have no other means of communicating their fears other than by extreme demanding behaviour – something you don't need when your nervous system is already in tatters. Make sure you take enough time out from your own preoccupations to check in with your children's. Keep in mind that even if your behaviour is bizarre and out of the ordinary it will still be providing your children with roles they may imitate.

I found my 8-year-old daughter quaffing painkillers in the bathroom. I said 'God what are you doing' and she said she was feeling bad. She had seen me palming down pills and thought she should too. I cleared the cabinet of all dangerous drugs straight away.

I thought we were behaving really well while he was in the throes of leaving. Then one day I noticed my younger son's schoolbook. His writing had become big and loopy and quite babyish. He was picking up all the suffering and charged atmospheres.

Older children might shout and swear at you and tell you they hate you. Roughly translated 'I hate you' means 'I don't understand why'. Shouting back might make you feel better, but it won't help your child. Just wait a bit until that particular storm has passed by and try to cope with the real message.

Adolescents are aware of a great deal more. They are in a testing time with their parents in any case – separated or together. They are exploring the limits of their own expanding world and going through huge physical and emotional charges.

At this age most normal children are fairly judgmental – however impeccable their parents' lives might be. When you are going through a curiously similar period of adjustment – new friends, a different pattern in your social life, lovers perhaps – your teenage children might turn out to be your strictest censors. Try not to resent that and make sure they know that what you are doing is all about getting on with your own life.

Take your teenage children into your confidence as much as

you can and treat their opinions and responses with an obvious respect. Direct conflict is pointless; teenage children are pretty skilful at getting in the last, guilt-provoking word when they feel you are vulnerable. Avoid putting unnecessary restrictions on your own life just through some fear of being judged by your children. Conquer the guilt, muster your courage and go in for a reasonable exchange of views instead.

I was dead scared about what the children would think if my new lover stayed overnight. We used to creep around like a pair of guilty teenagers. Eventually I saw how stupid it was and I asked them how they would feel if she stayed the night. My daughter just snorted and said she couldn't see any difference between that and her creeping home at dawn. My son thought it would be all right if I tidied my room and picked up the leaves – I realised I wasn't really dealing with children here at all, but young adults with their own view of the world, who would rather be asked than not and who actually cared that things were okay for me too.

The books I read when I was a girl were all set in rural-happy-family land – I can't remember any book that had an urban setting or a solo parent. My kids read amazing stuff now – strong mother images, working women, divorce, desertion. Through books and TV my kids have been exposed to the huge changes that have happened in society, much more than I ever was, or am now.

Remember that your children's world extends out beyond yours. They have a network of friends and social contacts that they will have to cope with in their changed state. Discuss their friend's reactions with them and try to provide solutions to any problems these might cause.

It is a good idea, particularly for younger children, to let their school teacher know the situation. This isn't a matter of baring your soul or secrets to some stranger, but simply a strategy to alert a person who spends a great deal of time with your child to the cause of any behaviour changes or problems.

The legal aspects of separated or divorced parents are covered in Chapter Seven. Usually one parent will have the day-to-day care and the day-to-day responsibility for the children, while the other will have contact at agreed times and for agreed periods. Both will share responsibility for the really big issues, about education or religion or health care for instance.

Both parents can have a split residence order and may take turns at living with the children in the family home, or the children may live for set periods with each parent. Whatever arrangement you make, try and see it from the point of view of the children. Split residence orders can, in some situations, be disturbing – if, for instance, the children have to move from home to home with two different sets of family arrangements to cope with.

If you have problems coming to some agreement about residence or contact then consider conciliation to help you sort something out between you. Your local Citizens' Advice Bureau will have details of services in your area. This, too, is covered in Chapter Seven. The best agreements are the ones you come to yourselves in the best interests of the children.

Sometimes to sort this out you have to put your own emotions aside — if you find this difficult, but feel you don't want or need formal or legal intervention then get a friend or relative to help.

I was absolutely livid! I had to ring my son about a birthday party while he was at his father's. Some teenager answered the phone and said she was the sitter and my bloody ex had gone off for the day to the cricket. I was speechless. Out of the two days he got to see the kids a fortnight he was off all day. I seethed and raged for the rest of the day winding myself up into a fine old fury. A friend brought me back to earth with the reminder that he was doing what he'd always done and if I hadn't changed that while I was married to him I wasn't going to do it now. As it turned out the kids had a marvellous day with the sitter and accepted their dad as he was.

There are some obvious things for the parent with whom the children normally live to avoid. Don't turn your children into secret agents in your ex's house. Avoid pressing them about personal details or the other parent's feelings. Don't make them feel out of line if they do bring such things up, but just steer the conversation on to easier ground.

Keep a regular check that any resentment you feel for the other parent doesn't spill over into how you manage their contact with the children. Never use that contact as a reward or punishment. Whatever your own feelings make sure the children don't get a message that their contact with their other parent causes you distress.

Keep the other parent involved with the big decisions. If

they live out of town keep them in touch with all the events in the children's lives and encourage the children to make that contact regular. If you were left on your own to tell the children, make sure the absent parent knows what they were told, how they received the news and what questions they asked. Do this even if you have to do it second-hand by letter through a solicitor.

No matter how bad your relations are with the other parent he or she must be informed of all problems relating to health, accidents or problem behaviours.

If your child has a confrontation with his or her other parent, either be supportive of the other parent or stay neutral – if you don't you may teach the child a lesson about manipulation that you will learn to regret.

As a parent with contact try and establish a regular schedule of contacts and stick to it. If you say you will turn up at a particular time make sure you do – you can be sure that your child will be waiting for you. Use as much of your time together to attend to the children as you can – especially if their visits are short.

If you live in another town, make sure you still keep in touch – keep those postcards and letters coming – and that your children know how to contact you.

Avoid the sugar-daddy or mummy approach and don't shower them with gifts or attention that might be seen by the other parent as bribery or an attempt to put them in an unfavourable light. Recognise that you will both have a different way of dealing with the child and a different quality of time together.

When differences do arise, just swallow your pride or discomfort and talk about them. If visits are causing genuine distress or behaviour problems, then try and sort out the real cause. If it is best for the child to give up the visits for a period, or treat them in a different way, then be prepared to face up to that.

I felt so hopeless watching my daughter. My two sons seemed to be okay . . . they enjoyed visiting their father. It upset my 10-year-old daughter. She bottled it up. Her posture changed – she sort of drooped. I saw her teacher at school – a wonderfully perceptive woman, herself separated. She was brilliant. For a while instead of silent reading, she got the kids doing silent writing. Apart from all the fantastic life histories she got from all the kids, we worked out that my daughter's misery was round her sense of betrayal of me when she went to her dad's. He had a new lady and she couldn't face the reality of me being dumped for somebody she didn't think was much chop. So for a while, with my husband's agreement, she didn't have to go there if she didn't want to. He sometimes saw her after school by herself, or picked her up from dancing – just short one-to-one meetings. After a couple of months she accepted the situation and started visiting again.

New partners, lovers, husbands, or wives can present children with some major problems. They can be straight-out resentful and defiant of the new person or just shut their feelings up in a glum silence. Don't push the relationship on them – let it grow at its own speed. Above all don't encourage them to see this new person as a substitute mother or father and to call the person Mum or Dad.

Let them see your happiness in the new relationship and be

open about it. This new adult in their life will take some getting used to, but if both you and they handle it well it can develop into a genuine supportive and caring friendship that does not challenge their feelings about the absent parent.

If you happen to be the absent parent keep in mind that it will not help your children if you encourage them to dislike the other person – they will only be confused about the other parent's real feelings and may worry about their own security with that parent.

The new relationship between yourself and your children is going to make a whole series of new demands on you. If you can't cope alone make sure you get some help.

I was amazed how easily my ex-husband could ask for help. He had scores of people lined up helping whereas I felt I should be able to cope on my own.

I remember noticing at work the women who looked anxiously out of the window if it rained, wondering if their kids had their coats or if the washing was getting wet. When I look back I don't know how I coped with the stress of those first couple of years learning to be a solo parent. Separated men don't seem to have those same reflexes – it got easier when I realised I could ask about things and that I didn't necessarily get treated with scorn for not knowing.

Grandparents can be a life saver, but they can also be very judgmental. Have a really frank discussion with them about just what is going on and how you would like them to help. As tactfully as you can, try to get them to hold off on expressing too much outrage.

Some mothers may initially lack mechanical skills and some fathers might collapse in a hopeless panic at a fever or a throw-up. Know your immediate limitations and have some idea of where help can be found if the fuses blow or if you draw a blank with getting a meal together that your children will actually eat.

If your children show any signs of stress or problem behaviour seek professional help immediately. Check with the school counsellor, your doctor or any other kind of help they or you may need. Check out the community resources for parents and children – you will be surprised at how many there are and how many children have been there before and survived.

If couples were really truthful, they don't really stay together for the sake of their children when their relationship cracks up. They stay together out of fear – of loneliness, or surviving on their own, of insecurity. They use their children as a tangible reason for staying together. I know. I stayed in a terrible marriage for six years after it was a marriage in name only. I know our staying together did my kids more harm. It was a loveless place and the atmosphere was grim. That's not good for children.

Both my ex-wife and I had pretty miserable childhoods. We had to get married young. We had kids too young. I blamed them for our problems and my ex blamed me. No, not a happy family. I think separating was best – not to keep a miserable family together like our parents had. We're all better friends now . . . matured.

CHAPTER SIX

Friends and False Friends;
Families and Ex-families

Right from the start I decided I wouldn't make a secret of it. I didn't feel ashamed or that I had anything to hide. In any case how are you going to start again on your own unless people know you're available? A few weeks after we had split up I was in the local dairy and some neighbours were there. I told them what had happened. Said they didn't need to get worried if my house seemed a bit quiet. That sort of thing. A couple of nights later there was a ring at the door and there was the lady neighbour. 'Oh ho!' I thought 'That's a bit quick'. But she said 'We're having a party on Saturday night and we thought you might like to come'. I thought that was really kind of them and asked if I could bring someone. 'Oh' she said 'we thought you'd be on your own, and there's this separated lady coming and, well, when she's had a few drinks she tends to get into the husbands and you could keep her busy'. I quickly found I had something else to do that Saturday night, but it was a pretty sharp lesson about how separated people are seen by couples and how they fit into some people's scheme of things.

. . . .

A widely reported experience of re-established single persons is the feeling that couples speak an entirely different language. Communicating some single experiences is nearly impossible. It is certainly difficult to establish amongst your married friends the notion that you are not necessarily an object of pity because you are single – nor are you constantly on the prowl to swap your single state, at any cost, for coupled bliss!

Some couples may see you as a threat, or at the very least as setting a dangerous example. Even the most sensitive of your couple friends will find it hard to grasp that your life now moves at a different pace from theirs.

At first you may find these responses hurtful or a strain, but your experience isn't theirs – you have moved into another kind of personal environment, while they remain in much the same place. Your relationship with the world is going to be more exposed, less shielded than theirs. What they see as unthinkable risks, you may happily accept as exciting challenges.

The simple process of getting your single life together again may seem to them as speeding recklessly along in the fast lane.

Some couple friends may fade out of your life. They may find your new lifestyle too much of a threat, or they may have been friends of the relationship rather than the individuals in it. It may be that they were closer to your partner, or that they found their loyalties too stretched by seeing either.

Your split may have made them fearful of strains in their own relationship. It may even be that your misery was just too much for them, or you asked for more support than they could give.

Whatever the reason, friendships with other couples will inevitably be reassessed. Some will survive. Others will have gone forever. A few will come back or survive your new relationship with them – even these will be adjusted to the changes in your life.

It sort of sets up a strange imbalance when someone absconds from the couples' circuit. Wives feel nervous in case it is contagious, husbands feel a bit restless and either become very self-righteous or find their eyes roving. Some even turn up at the deserted wife's door with a bottle of wine and think she might like a bit of the other too. Your split will cause a ripple around your married friends – you can bet they'll examine their own marriages and close ranks.

Bit by bit I found that I was living an entirely different lifestyle from my married friends. I was astonished, for instance, to find that they knew nothing of our city's nightlife – it had changed amazingly for the better during our marriages while we, unaware, stayed snug in our suburban nests. Their life seemed so slow. I called them the waltzing turtles.

The shock, misery and, perhaps, public humiliation of your separation has propelled you into an entirely different universe from that inhabited by couples. Cocooned in habit and routine their world seems essentially different to yours, where habit and routine have given way to challenge. In short, their lives will seem, in fact are, duller than yours. Some of them, who have detected this possibility, may resent you for it.

You may be lonely in your newly single state, but at the

same time you will also be overwhelmed by the busyness of the real world outside your relationship. The walls have gone. What once, before your separation, was a view seen through a window has become a bustling reality in which, willingly or not, you have become a bustling participant.

To your couple friends you may be irritatingly full of a new vigour and restlessness. In the moments you spare from your grieving, you will almost certainly be full of plans – plans which can shift and readjust from moment to moment, zipping from simple to grandiose in the space of a sentence. Your married friends, on the other hand, have, at least on the visible surfaces of their relationship, settled their plans light years ago. They will be fretful in the face of the new while you – if you are on the path of becoming single – will be hopelessly full of enthusiasm for it.

As best you can, don't let all these altered states put your old friendships with couples at risk, but by the same token don't allow them to dampen your re-emergence into the world either. Accept that the relationship has changed, that the languages you speak have subtly moved away from each other, and that your new singleness may be as challenging for some of your friends as it is for you.

The longer you have been in your relationship, the more likely it is that your friends will also be married or in stable partnerships. Close friends will most likely have detected your problems very early in the piece. You may have already discussed it with one or other of them or at least sent out signals of the gathering storm.

While you may not realise it at first, all the differences

between your new state and that of your couple friends will begin to show up almost as soon as the separation. Try to keep them in mind, when you are relating to couples you need and would like to stay close to.

Suddenly I seemed to become a non-person. I would meet old friends at the shops, who would be full of sympathy and interest, but who quickly got furtive if it came to discussing their social life. I quickly realised that a single person is not much of an asset in the cosy dinner party circuit of couples. I realised it was because a single woman is seen as an instant threat to other women's husbands or lovers. I was angry at first, but as I got to meet other single-again people I realised it was a common experience and that separated men suffered it too, if in a slightly different version. One male friend told me that he felt he was on a kind of stud farm – called on to service dangerous single women!

Couple friends who have slipped out of your life – probably unnoticed – may surface from time to time when they contemplate a 'difficult' single guest for a social occasion. They think in 'couples' and can only imagine being single as an uncomfortable space in between. Try not to knock all their invitations – it is at least one way of meeting new people.

When the bust-up finally happens old friends can provide an essential support system to carry you through the first shock and denial phase of your grieving. It is important that you take enough time out of your misery to make sure you are not putting this system on to overload.

Don't expect your friends to feel things as intensely as you do. Don't demand that they take sides – they may, but that will be their decision and one they may make for entirely different reasons.

In your rage at your absent partner, you may be tempted to use your friends as a weapon in the war you imagine has been declared. You may use your friendship as a blackmailing device to bully them into falling out of friendship with the ex. Don't do it. You will either place your friendship under an intolerable strain or lose it entirely.

The sympathy of your friends, their love and support, are not necessarily declarations on their part that they will also share your anger and burning desire for revenge or punishment. The fact they they will see your separation in an entirely different perspective to your own can be an invaluable asset in helping you get yourself and the world into a softer focus.

Make sure you do not load your friends with your problems to the exclusion of everything else. Their patience and sympathy may wear fairly thin if you stay stuck in misery. Make sure you have other things to talk about and take time to be a listener – they may have problems they need you for.

Gradually the grey fog will clear and the outside world will become more interesting than your own emotional state. Another very common experience of those in the process of becoming single is the discovery of a new intensity about the world outside their relationship. It can be a bit like the difference between the sudden heightening of perceptions that goes with swapping a black-and-white television for colour.

Some friends who stay close to both after the split can actually do more harm than good. It is hard to confide your feelings to someone who may very well be passing on your feelings to your ex. Or you may find the temptation to use them to pass on angry or painful messages almost too much to resist.

Other friends may feel uncertain about their own feelings and while loving you dearly may not be able to cope with all the emotional squalls you are steering them into. Rather than blaming this sort of friend for being a piker or the other kind for being a fifth columnist, just leave them until things have settled. If you value their friendship make a new approach to them later, when you feel able to cope.

Depending on how public your bust-up was, you may find that quite a few people you hardly knew, suddenly take an interest in your well-being. Many of these are well meaning and have impeccable intentions. Others are not and you may feel you are taking a part in some private novel or play.

All sorts of people came to see me when my husband ran off with our neighbour's wife, whom I had thought was my friend. Huh! Because it was all so local and community minded, women I didn't know very well came round to talk and unburden their own unsatisfactory life stories on me. There is a ghoulish curiosity too. People want to see what it is like with no 'cut' and 'cut to handsome stranger' like on TV. And they wanted to tell me awful stories about my ex that I didn't want to hear. I began to feel as if my house was a shrine to consciousness raising. I got busy very quickly. You can do without all that heart and brain surgery in your own living room.

For your own protection you need to learn quickly how to sort out real friends from the false. Your recovery will not be helped by gossiping acquaintances who want to give you 'news' about the departed or tell you past wickednesses that they 'always thought you should know'.

Such 'friends' are dangerous and should be firmly, but kindly, cut off at the knees. So too should 'friends' who, in the guise of lending a sympathetic ear, encourage you to indulge your misery or negative feelings for their own perverse enjoyment.

For a lot of unhappy people, your misfortune will be like a marital traffic accident put on for their entertainment. Like the bothersome gawkers at the scene of an accident such people should be quickly moved on.

Newly single women may also attract the unhealthy attentions of their female friends' husbands. Some men feel that their sexual come-ons are doing the separated woman a favour. Some may just be misguided and insensitive men who actually mean no harm and can be gently and easily dealt with. Others, more predatory, might present more of a problem.

If such men persist, suggestions that their company will only be welcome with that of their wives or lovers can sometimes get the message across. You may need to ask bluntly if their partner knows where they are, or suggest that if they call again you may find it necessary to let her know where they are.

One chap, whose wife had been a friend of mine for years, got into the habit of 'popping in' to see if I was okay and if I needed help with anything around the house. I was grateful at first, but he soon made it obvious that the house wasn't all he intended to 'pop in' to. The last straw was when he turned up in the middle of the night, half-cut, and tried to grope me. He was abject when I finally got loose and dead scared that I would tell his wife – the threat of that was enough to keep him away after that. I feel uncomfortable when I am around them both, but I didn't want to lose her supportive friendship.

After the first phase of your separation, you may find that keeping your circle of friends intact will demand some effort on your part. Make sure you keep in touch – the good times as well as the times you are feeling rotten.

Your misery is no excuse for forgetting friends' birthdays, or anniversaries, or for not taking part in their celebrations. Nor have you been excused from returning some of the hospitality you are given. It may take some time to get that together, but making a cake or sharing a bottle of wine takes no great effort.

I hated the weekends – Sundays particularly. I would sit around waiting for friends to turn up. Of course few of them did. It didn't occur to me that I had to make some effort. One weekend I pulled myself together and asked a couple I had been close to around for lunch. It was a great success – not the lunch, which was what you would expect from a newly singled bloke – but just having people in the flat. I had felt like some sort of leper, but it was my own fault. My friends were getting on with their ordinary lives and needed an invitation into mine. I think they thought I spent my weekends in wicked bachelor sinfulness and wouldn't need them around!

New friends can sometimes present some problems to your old. Particularly new lovers. Just treat these encounters with some tact. You may feel tempted to show off your ability to attract new attention from the opposite sex, but it can sometimes be a little heavy-handed to do it to your married friends.

There may be an element of jealousy or they may simply be uncomfortable with your showing affection to a stranger. If they are a couple they may feel slightly threatened by your ability to begin a new relationship.

I would chatter away to my close friends – couples of course – about my new loves and rush them into a lunch with them or some other kind of social encounter. Some coped very well and others didn't – at the mention of this new, fabulous woman their eyes would roll. 'Here he goes again'. It took me a little while to sort out the friends who wanted to hear and those who didn't. The first lot were pretty good at relating to new people in my life and the others were not, but both were still my friends – I just had to do things differently with each.

Try not to force new relationships on old friends. Ease them into it and let them know exactly how you feel about the new person. Your new friend may feel slightly uncomfortable too. It will be hard for them to feel that your friends are not comparing them with the ex. If they feel strongly for you, they may also feel just a little jealous of the past time you have shared with your friends.

Tuning into these emotions is good therapy. It will certainly strengthen your relationships with both old and new friends.

If circumstances have separated you from your friends – you may have moved to another town for instance – you may still need someone close to confide in. Making new friends can take a little time.

If you feel you are going to need somebody to talk to in a crisis, or even just somebody to talk to about quite small problems, approach your local voluntary agencies. The Yellow Pages in your telephone book will list them. You may just need to know about social groups, sport clubs, cultural societies or adult classes. A citizens' advice bureau will have access to a stack of these. These organisations are there to help. They understand the problems of people who are isolated from family or friends.

Lifeline stresses that no problem is too small. Quite ordinary things can sometimes seem like major problems without some outside input to put them into focus. If you feel you need help and advice, ask for it.

My own parents are dead and my only brother lives overseas, but we started writing to each other which has been wonderful. My ex-in-laws have never been in touch at all, never contact their grandchildren. At first I used to send letters from the kids with photos and drawings, but I've given up and put all my energy into making a new life for us, with the help of a few, good, old, pre-marriage friends. We're doing well.

Our social conditioning encourages us to see the break-up of a marriage – even a rotten marriage – as a failure of some sort; failure of love to endure; a failure of some people's response to change; a failure to cope with and come through hard times.

Separation challenges the old happily-ever-after ending we have been indoctrinated with from birth. Perhaps this has lessened a little in our times, where society is slowly accepting the high level of separation and divorce as nothing unusual.

Certainly our divorce laws are a great deal more humane, less judgmental and less strewn with legal obstacles than those which confronted our parents.

Old attitudes to divorce, however, still endure. Parents sometimes find the separation of their children difficult to accept and they may be more ready to apportion fault and blame them than the partners themselves.

I was so afraid of telling my parents we had split up that we went through a whole Christmas charade together rather than admit it. He couldn't tell his parents either. We were both terrified of their reactions because they had helped us so much, financially . . . you know, they had a lot invested in us. There were dreadful scenes too, when we finally did tell. Why didn't we 'stick it out' (like they had). 'What will we tell so and so?' 'We've never had a divorce in the family'. It too so much courage to tell them and phenomenal strength to put up with the wrath.

My parents adored my wife. I think they loved her more than me, their own son. When we separated they just dismissed me and gave all their support to her. It was a relief in one way, but terribly hurtful in another.

Most parents feel hurt and angry that the smooth surface of kinship and family has been broken. They may feel that they have failed or that their help and support to the marriage has been spurned.

Some parents might dread the idea that a daughter, dumped with small children, might want to move back home and disrupt their hard-earned child-free days. They may feel cheated that a son or daughter-in-law they once thought so charming has turned out a rotter.

If the marriage was childless they may hurl accusations of selfishness for not having the children that would have 'kept the marriage together'. If there are children they may feel equally resentful that their grandchildren 'haven't been taken into account'.

It would be unnatural if parents did not have feelings about your bust-up. Their feelings about the separation will probably be in proportion to the hopes they had invested in the relationship in the first place. Their family pride may well be hurt and they may feel a sense of failure.

I reacted very Old Testament to my son-in-law leaving my daughter. I wanted to cut off his head, but I cut him out of my life instead. I felt if he had left my daughter he had to leave us too. I felt strongly about our family and if he wanted out he had to accept that included us too. I know he loved us dearly and my daughter had to work hard on me to relent.

It is important, of course, to be sensitive to these feelings, but it is also important that you avoid adding their responses to your own emotional problems. The last thing you want in the initial trauma of separation is the feeling that you have let somebody else down.

Explain to your parents – and to your ex's if they are still in the picture – exactly how you are feeling and what is happening. Let them know you need their love and support and that any post-mortems can be postponed until later. Tell them how they can help you in your new status. Encourage them to accept the separation as a fact and let them know that any anger or bitterness they feel about the situation is not very helpful. You can even ask for them to help shut you up if you harp on along the same lines.

Helpful and sympathetic parents can be an invaluable asset in the process of recovery. Intolerant and judgmental parents are best kept at a distance – no matter how much you love them. After all, it is your life and future that is being reorganised.

I was amazed at my mother when my marriage broke up. She helped me so much, it seemed to give her a new lease on life. At first I was a bit nervous at being squeezed back into some daughterly mould, but it was quite the reverse – she wanted to help me get out of one and into the world again.

My wife's family was absolutely tribal – matriarchal as well. When we split I was simply dismissed from the tribal consciousness. It was more than if I had died; it was as if I had never existed. I didn't mind too much. I had felt an outsider most of the time anyway, but it was hard on the children who had this extra pressure to cope with and who had to put up with a thin-lipped, hostile granny if they incautiously mentioned their father.

Grandparental disapproval can be particularly hard on grand-children. It puts a further strain on their loyalties and adds to their confusion and unhappiness. It is important to explain to your parents, and get your ex to explain to theirs, that your children are not being helped by them sounding off about the shortcomings of their mum and dad.

It is important that children keep in touch with both lots of grandparents. A full set of loving grandparents can help them through the fears and worries they may have about their parents. If the grandparents can't provide support, then it is best to restrict access to their grandchildren until the emotional environment is more settled.

My children adored their father's parents, but his mother was so angry about our separation. The first holiday they stayed with her she ripped into me to them and the next time they went it was his turn – she switched loyalties and lammed into her darling son. They didn't want to go back for ages. She kept saying things like 'You're just like your father (or mother)', disparagingly, so they felt bad too. It particularly affected my daughter who was fourteen and worried about her looks. She was the dead spit of her father – hearing all those criticisms of him made her feel she might be a bad egg too.

Your separation will put considerable strains on your family and friends. The closer they are, the closer they are likely to feel it. Most of them will come up trumps if you take care to nurture the relationship and let them know that whatever you are feeling you value it. Accept that the changes in your life will mean changes for your friends and family too.

Becoming single can strengthen your existing network of relationships. It can bring new friendships and it can deepen old ones. There will be losses and gains. Things will never be the same as they were. They may well be better.

A couple of years after the separation I decided to ask all the friends I felt really close to, to a big thank you party. I was amazed at just how many old friends had stuck by me – through all my demands and my tantrums. Some of them were still close to my ex-wife, but that seemed okay. I was also astonished at how many new friends I had made – friends I felt genuine love for and whom I might never have met had I stayed married. I tried to make a thank you speech, but just burst into tears instead. That was greeted with cheers and hugs and one friend said, 'You couldn't have done that two years ago'. He was right and I was glad that I could now.

CHAPTER SEVEN

Alone at Last

Looking back, it's obvious that music was one of the things we didn't have in common. Because of that I'd sort of filtered it out of my life. I thought I listened to it, but really I didn't very much. When she took the records, that seemed fair enough – they were nearly all hers anyway. Then I started to miss a bit of music in the house and I went down to the record shop and started to pull out all the old familiar things – 'respectable' classics: Bach, Mozart and so on. Then I thought 'Hang on. Why these?' So I pushed them back and pulled out things I wouldn't have dreamed of listening to before – Berlioz, Mahler, Satie and the like. Suddenly there was a whole new world of music that prejudice or laziness, or a shared taste, had shut me off from. It was a real revelation and I thought 'If I can discover something like that about music, what about the rest of my life? Food. Different sorts of people. Different places. You don't have to go on repeating yourself. You didn't ask for a new start, but you've got one anyway so why not make the most of it?'

I can't stand the time between the end of work and going to sleep. I forget a lot at work — but having to go back to the house, the kids for company, trying to keep going. It's like being becalmed — everyone else planning holidays, organising their lives, but mine seems so directionless at the moment. I drink a lot. The kids hate it. I have to have some sort of anaesthetic. And I know I'm so fragile when I do go out and I can't enjoy myself — seeing other loving couples makes me cry.

. . . .

After love and sex, loneliness must rank as the third great preoccupation of the human race. It is the theme of some of the greatest novels, poems, plays and paintings. From the moment we first open our eyes, to when we finally close them, we are, or yearn to be, part of a gregarious society. Humans are social animals and being part of a tribe or a family or some other group, is their natural condition. Being thrown out is a serious punishment. The outcast is universally despised and the refugee universally pitied.

Loneliness is also one of humanity's greatest illusions. Whether we are part of a group or not, ultimately we all live alone in our individual world of feeling. Of course we reach out from that, and we share our feelings and we are enriched by sharing the feelings of others — that after all is what art is basically for; to enable individual experience to be shared and expressed and understood.

No matter how close we feel to others and how strong our sense of belonging is, our strongest inner feeling is one of being alone. That particular feeling produces some of our worst fears and anxieties and is sometimes our greatest source of strength.

The first and often the worst blow struck by separation, is that our inner feeling of aloneness has become an external reality. Someone whom we believed understood our feelings and with whom it was easiest, or so we thought, to share and express them has cast us aside. We were part of something and now we are not.

I was told by a friend, who had also been divorced, that until you've learned to manage by yourself – which of course means coping with feeling lonely sometimes – you'll never really be able to live with anyone else. He was right. I'd tried leaping straight into a so-called love affair, clutching this person, trying to blot out my desolation, but it was hopeless. But lonely feelings are like tiredness or the blues. They don't last forever. They do go.

It has been said the loneliness is basically a sense of failure. In a gregarious world being alone is a stigma. If we don't have somebody else or if we are not obviously part of a group then there must be something wrong with us.

These feelings run very deep – they probably begin in our childhood with our first encounter with groups outside our immediate family – and they are difficult to come to terms with easily or to put aside. Of even earlier origin and running even deeper, is the idea that loneliness is basically a yearning for the time when we were physically a part of our mothers.

I found myself staring at couples, resenting them for their togetherness while I was alone. I got quite paranoid about it and started to feel like a bit of a peeping tom or a dirty old man, I was so intense in my awareness of couples – what did they have that I didn't? It was all very silly and all very childish, but I couldn't help those feelings at first.

My mother died when I was 8. I can remember aching with loneliness, longing for her, and my father being so remote. At 18 I railroaded my boyfriend into marriage. I was a real limpet – totally dependent. When we split up it was my mother I kept crying for.

The first thing to grasp about loneliness is that it is a feeling that anyone can experience regardless of their situation – separated or in the closest relationship. Many rotten relationships provide for one or both of the partners some desperate moments of loneliness. So do many successful relationships as well.

Many people leave a relationship rather than endure the loneliness within it. It is true, too, that an equally large number of people endure a bad or dead marriage rather than face being alone. But being alone and being lonely are not the same thing. Getting hold of that idea is one of the best therapies the newly separated can experience. 'I am alone, but I am not lonely.' Write it down somewhere.

Of course you will feel lonely some of the time – perhaps even most of the time at first – but so do most people. Your loneliness might seem the final straw, when it piles in on top of all the other aspects of upheaval and destruction following the great divide. It is awful having no-one to confide in, particularly when an instinctive reference to the other person is one of the things we all miss most when our relationship goes on the rocks. You have every reason to feel more than a little sorry for yourself, but don't use that as an excuse to start on a descending spiral of self-pity.

Being alone has just as many positive aspects as it does negative. On a purely selfish level, being alone means you can please yourself. So long as that doesn't become a reason for self-neglect, it is a luxurious opportunity for self-indulgence that few couples enjoy.

I'd never lived by myself ever. I was 43 and had never been alone in my house – or anyone else's house – before. I came from a big family, married from home at 20, and had always been used to being with family. I couldn't believe the luxury of deciding for myself what to do next – if anything! I found it hard going out by myself though. It took a year before I could go to town and have lunch by myself. I felt so self-conscious alone in public.

Draw up a list of all the things that you would consider pampering yourself. They don't have to be major extravagances – just simple things like a bunch of flowers in the bedroom or a bottle of good white wine for a weekend lunch. Treat yourself to something from the list at least once a week and more if you can afford the time or expense. Night-time and sleep are problem areas for many newly separated people, so perhaps your self-indulgence can extend to something associated with those things. Is your pillow luxurious enough for instance? What about an electric blanket or a new duvet cover? Do you enjoy a really delicious cup of tea or hot chocolate in bed? Do you like to listen to music in bed or watch television or scatter the bed with books and magazines or eat biscuits or hot buttered toast? You can spoil yourself, be a pig, sprawl over the whole bed and no-one will judge or resent you for it. That is one very obvious asset in being alone!

It is probably true about the big expenses in life and the long-term household economy, that two can live more cheaply than one, but it is also true that it costs one less to have a luxury from time to time than it does for two.

Pampering doesn't extend only to material things. You can behave like a child if you want and be thoroughly unpredictable. You can experiment with wearing a different style of clothes or eating different foods at different times. You can go to bed at five or at midnight or not got to bed at all. You can behave outrageously and sing at the top of your voice in the shower.

You can afford to be curious about the world. You can do whatever you want, even things that are completely out of character. You may or may not like them, but they will certainly give you something new to think about.

You may not have asked for this new freedom, or even wanted it, but now you have it, it would be the height of folly not to try it out. Be thoroughly honest with yourself and ask if you ever had this much potential for change and chance within your relationship. It would have been a very unusual relationship if you had.

When I took my kids out to the pool, I decided to join them going down the hydro-slide. My usual role is to sit buttering the bread and do the picnic food. Well! The kids' faces! My face! The first ride was terrifying. I screamed my head off. It was a riot. The child in me rose to the occasion. I felt great.

I seldom bought clothes or shoes without consulting my wife. She had her ideas about how people like me dressed and I went along with them — sort of conservative — a cross between her father, who was a provincial businessman, and the architects in our group, who she thought were quite daring. As a result I shuffled about in corduroy trousers, viyella shirts and clumpy suede shoes. Yuck! The very first time I started looking at men's fashions and how I wanted to dress, free from her influence, I realised I had spent my marriage locked up in a sartorial prison — and what a joy it was to buy a pair of shoes I didn't actually need without feeling any guilt.

Feelings of emotional insecurity can heighten anxieties about physical security. If you are not used to being alone and especially if you are having problems sleeping, your house at night can sometimes seem frightening. Those creaks and squeaks that you took for granted when you had the comfort of another adult, warm and close by, can take on an ominous character.

It is best not to just lie there night after night, turning your house or flat into some personal ghost train or horror film. Check your household security out. Make sure you feel secure in your home. Establish a routine for locking up and if you are doubtful about how secure your house is, get some professional advice.

Your local locksmith will give good advice on locks and window catches. Try checking with your community constable and let him or her know you are alone, or alone with your children. If there is an existing neighbourhood watch group, then get on its files and let your local coordinator and immediate neighbours know your situation. If there isn't an existing group then see about starting one up.

Neighbourhood support, the police, or any security firm in the Yellow Pages will give you advice about alarm systems if you feel you need to install one. These range from quite complicated set-ups to a simple siren and outside light system set off by a bedside panic button.

If you do have an alarm system, again make sure your neighbours know. Even without the expense of installing some system, you and your neighbours can agree on help signals with lights, whistles, or those portable aerosol sirens that boat owners buy for fog horns.

The important thing is to feel secure. Once you do, those bumps and creaks in the dark can go back to being the comfortable sounds of your house settling down for the night that they were when you weren't alone.

If you are a woman alone, then you might feel your security is improved by doing a self-defence course. The local neighbourhood watch coordinator or citizens' advice bureau will direct you to a suitable course.

Every step you take towards becoming self-sufficient will be one more boost to your morale. Maybe for the first time in your life you will have to be totally responsible for yourself and for your actions. You will begin progressively to feel more and more in control of your own life. There are few feelings more exhilarating than the awareness of personal freedom that comes from challenging and overcoming your fears about managing alone.

A new lease on life is a phrase that will come to have a whole new meaning. Make the most of it. Every step you take along this path will make you a more self-reliant and more attractive person. The world does not love a wimp!

The good thing about all this is just how much of it is in your control. Of course it may take a huge conscious effort to develop a positive attitude about being on your own, particularly in periods of emotional storm. But it is important to start early in seeing the advantages of having time to yourself, rather than restlessly wandering around wondering what you might be missing.

It is a good strategy to start a diary – at least no-one else will read it! Writing down your progress day by day is a good way to monitor it and it is also a very pleasant diversion, not unlike having a conversation with a close friend who understands exactly how you feel.

If you always want to be out with other people or have some-one constantly around, it may mean you have no confidence in yourself. This is a natural enough response to the trauma of splitting up, but it is not a condition you can afford to make permanent. A good sense of self-esteem is essential to recovery, and self-reliance and self-esteem are natural allies.

My father rented me an answerphone which turned out to be an incredible blessing. I'd had a few crank calls which had upset me very much. I depended so much on the phone too, and had got into that silly cycle of waiting for new men to ring. Sometimes I'd not go out at all if someone said they would ring and nine times out of ten they wouldn't! With the answerphone I could go out and not worry. It was great for kids too, being able to leave messages for me and for each other and contact numbers. I also used to leave it on if I didn't feel like talking – a great liberation.

For a person alone and for an adult living alone with their children, a simple machine like a telephone-answering device can provide an immense sense of freedom. Mainly it is freedom from fears of missing out on something, but even that is a pretty important release. Be careful though, if you do use an answering machine, not to make it a dent in your security. Leave neutral messages and don't be too specific about the length of time you intend to be out.

Going out, or rather, coming home after being out, can often provide the single person with some of their more acute feelings of loneliness. As times like these, in the transitional space between being in company and being alone, negative feelings about your situation are likely to crowd in.

I had a terrible fear about going home alone. I'd do anything to put off the evil hour. That was the worst time for me – that awful facing of my lonely flat. Lonely me.

If you are prone to such feelings it is a good idea to make sure that your flat or house will be welcoming. Leave the radio playing softly. Leave the bedside light on and your electric blanket on. Put some flowers by the bed. Turn that empty space into a welcoming nest that is waiting to cosset you.

It may be that a few bad nights are inevitable. These times are probably going to be among some of your most critical, so make sure you have developed some coping strategies in advance.

I was okay during the day, but once the kids were in bed and I had a long night to face alone, I nearly went crazy. It was like a radio – you know how at night you can get so many more stations and the radio waves are stronger – so even though my body was tired, my brain went into overdrive.

It is a good idea to make sure there is a tolerant friend at the other end of the telephone for black moments like these. Talkback radio is a good reminder that the world is full of people who need someone else to talk to and if things really do get desperate, then there is Lifeline or the Samaritans to ring and talk to.

Loneliness can induce thoughts of suicide. Such notions are natural enough and sooner or later, when you are feeling lonely and unable to cope, you are bound to give them a passing glance or even a hard look. Suicidal thoughts are almost always a signal that you want help – sometimes they are even a bizarre strategy for revenge on the person who has hurt you. Don't ignore the signals. Confront your feelings and get yourself back into focus or get outside help immediately you feel yourself sliding down this particular path. There are less lethal ways of getting help – a single phone call to Lifeline for instance. Lifeline and similar telephone numbers can be found in the Yellow Pages of your phone book.

The American poet Dorothy Parker had some good cautionary things to say to people contemplating suicide.

> 'Razors pain you;
> Rivers are damp.
> Acids stain you;
> And drugs cause cramp.
> Guns aren't lawful;
> Nooses give;
> Gas smells awful.
> You might as well live.'

Many attempted suicides cause themselves permanent injury. Far from lethal doses of drugs can cause permanent and disabling kidney and liver damage. Few things can be more degrading than having one's stomach pumped out. And as a signal to the errant lover suicide is a pretty useless and empty gesture.

My worst moment came in the middle of a long weekend — probably that was the reason, everyone else was on holiday and I was trapped alone, wallowing in my misery. I got all the pills I could find in the house and lined them up. Then for the first time I realised that I had to have outside help — that my stubborn determination to cope entirely alone was really just crass stupidity. I threw all the pills in the rubbish, poured myself an enormous drink and rang an old friend who had been trying to get me to see a counsellor.

Holidays and festive occasions can provide powerful triggers for feelings of loneliness. If you are in the habit of celebrating your birthday, then there is no reason to give it up simply because you are single again. Invite friends or family to a celebration at home or arrange an evening out with them. Christmas and New Year celebrations are times you should also plan carefully, well in advance.

Long weekends can stretch out to an immensely long misery if you haven't planned for them. If you are a custodial parent, these are most likely to be the times your children are with the other parent. Don't mope, give yourself a holiday and indulge the time you have free for yourself.

Entertaining is a marvellous cure for the blues. If you haven't cooked before, then learning how to can be a wonderfully distracting adventure.

My wife left and took all the cookery books and most of the utensils with her, so I enrolled for some nightclass cooking lessons on Middle Eastern food. I've never enjoyed myself more. It was a whole unexplored side of me and I couldn't believe how creative cooking could be. I was still the walking wounded so for me the joy of cooking was far more healing than the joy of sex.

There are a number of excellent recipe books for solo cooks or for dishes that will feed two. If your culinary skills are limited it is probably best to extend them in these more modest directions at first and work up to large scale dinner parties. Cooking can be such a rewarding pastime that it is well worthwhile not to scare yourself off it at the beginning by tackling menus that are too ambitious.

If you are a mother left with children, cooking might well

be the last thing you want to think about. Try to involve your children in shopping and cooking. Plan group dinners with friends at the weekend to share the burden and as well provide some economic socialising. If the budget runs to it, eat out at least once a month.

Being alone at last may offer you a whole new set of challenges and a chance to learn entirely new skills. You may not have managed money before and will need to in a sometimes tighter economic climate. You can get budgeting advice from your local citizens' advice bureau if you need it. It is a good idea if you are new to managing finances to keep a detailed record of where the money goes. You may never have done the ironing before or have no idea about how to manage the simplest of household tasks. Getting to grips with these can provide quite a disproportionate amount of self-respect.

My GP told me a terrible story about a widow he encountered, who was in the dark every night because she had no ideal how to change the light bulbs and didn't want to take the risk. I laughed, but it made me think about all the things I had some secret doubts about tackling round the house. I went home determined to make a list of all the things I thought I couldn't do and find out how to do them.

Some English wit, perhaps it was Oscar Wilde, described marriage as being like a beleaguered fortress with those on the inside trying to get out and those on the outside trying to get in. Being single could be seen in the same ironic way. In a relationship or out, there are good, rewarding times and miserable times.

It may seem a bit of a cliché, but it is useful to reflect that everybody's life is a balance between joys and sorrows with heaps of neutral bits in the middle. Being alone can be a burden, but it can also be a blessing. If you seize the challenges being alone offers it can become a marvellous opportunity to do quite a bit of growing as a person.

I still feel great pangs of feeling alone, even five years after my divorce. At first the sad days way outnumbered the good ones, but that passed. Now I find I have more depth of feeling than I did. My sad days are sadder and my good days – the majority now – are profoundly more happy. I am so much more alive. It took a lot of time and a lot of courage.

I thought I would never manage even the simplest things about looking after myself, but once I had struggled through that feeling of uselessness and tackled the ironing and the housework (things I thought I did my share of, but had only been fooling myself about) I found that even these mundane things were a chance to have my life the way I wanted it – to set standards and be proud to keep them. Then I had the courage to approach cooking and what a wonderful world I found there. Maybe I will get into a relationship again, marry perhaps, but being alone holds no fears any more and I reckon I'm ten times the human being I was.

CHAPTER EIGHT

The Law

I really loved my wife. I had accepted that she wasn't coming back and I resented that, and I resented her for the pain and sense of failure and loss I had. I was even very angry with her from time to time. More than that I suppose I even felt I could despise her for what she had done to me. But I didn't hate her – until I got the first letter from her solicitor. I certainly hated her then. How could she do this to me after all the pain, rejection, grief and whatever else? To add to that, these cruel and heartless demands, far, far beyond anything she could possibly believe was fair or just. Then I realised that she hadn't. The letter wasn't from her. It was from her solicitor and he didn't give a stuff about me and why should he? When I got my solicitor I told him I didn't want to go down that road and we didn't.

He had always been able to get the better of me in arguments and I knew I wasn't likely to win this one – especially since his pride was so hurt. I tried to talk to him about the house and about the children, but it would just end up in a bitter shouting match. I wanted to get on with my life so I went to a solicitor to sort things out. I had never been to a solicitor on my own before and I was apprehensive about it. She was good – really good. She steered me away from all the emotional tangles and helped me see exactly where I stood, what my rights were and what the law said I was entitled to. Just as well too, since my guilt about the whole bust-up had made me feel I wasn't really entitled to anything.

. . . .

Beneath all the romantic symbolism of marriage – the vows, the ring, the assembled guests and beaming relatives – lies a straightforward legal contract. If your relationship was a marriage, you made a whole series of commitments which the law obliges you to keep. Even if your relationship was not a formal marriage, if you owned property or a business together, or if you had children, then that kind of relationship too might have some legal obligations.

The legal path into marriage has very few obstacles. The other end of the process is considerably more formidable. Getting into the contract may have seemed easy; getting out is often a very hard and painful road through a legal minefield. The trip can often be made even more difficult than it actually is, by the emotional smokescreens that obscure the way.

Generally there is no need to rush into the legal aspects of breaking up. You may be pushed by the other partner or you may just want to get it over with and get on with your life. In either case make sure you take enough time to know exactly what you are doing. Be certain that your judgment is not clouded by pain or guilt.

Getting a broad idea of your legal rights, however, is simple commonsense. Places where you can obtain general information are a Citizens' Advice Bureau or a law centre. At the very least, these organisations should have available the latest pamphlets on all aspects of separation and divorce.

There is only one ground on which you can obtain a divorce – the irretrievable breakdown of your marriage. However, the court will require you to prove one of five factual situations, or 'facts'. The first three of these facts depend on the other party (the respondent as he or she is called in the divorce) having either committed adultery, or other unreasonable behaviour, or deserted you for at least two years. If you both want a divorce you can divorce after two years' separation, provided the respondent consents to the divorce. If your spouse is unwilling to consent to a divorce and has not done anything to enable you to bring a divorce on the first three facts, the only ground will be five years' separation.

If your spouse has committed adultery you do not need to name the person with whom he or she has committed it or make them a party to the divorce. However you do need to prove that, as a result either of the adultery or of any other behaviour of the other party, you find it intolerable to go on living with them.

If your spouse has behaved badly you can bring a divorce based on their unreasonable behaviour and that as a result of this you cannot reasonably be expected to go on living with them. The behaviour could be violence, or other misconduct or neglect, or just the accumulation of a whole series of incidents.

When you separate you do not have to make a formal legal declaration that you have separated. Separation begins when one partner leaves the home and decides that the marriage is over. This makes a legal separation even if the other partner wants to go on with the marriage. There must, however, be a conscious decision by one partner that the marriage is over; you would not be legally separated, and able to apply for a divorce after two or five years, if you had lived apart because of work or other reasons.

Under some circumstances, if it is impossible for one of you to move out, you can separate under the same roof if one of you moves into a separate bedroom and it is clear that the relationship is over in all other respects. You will normally have to produce independent evidence that this is so and anyone thinking of following this course of action should get legal advice.

The law does enable you to attempt a reconciliation without prejudicing the fact, so long as the period you spend living together before the divorce does not total more than six months. Despite this, in separation cases the time spent living together cannot count towards the two or five year period needed as grounds for divorce. Isolated instances of making love during this time usually make no difference either.

STORM WARNINGS

Very few people go into a marriage or live-in relationship with the idea that it isn't going to last. Obviously they are not going to tie any matrimonial knot while planning how it might be unravelled at some time in the future. The marriage is a contract, however, and whatever the loving couple might have planned for it, the law takes into account what will happen if the contract comes unstuck and it sets out a simple series of steps for unsticking it when the time comes.

Some couples will draw up an agreement about property and other things before they get married, but these realistic or cautious couples are very much in the minority. In any event, such contracts may not be recognised by the court.

Quite a few relationships blow apart without any obvious warnings. Either one partner simply was unaware of what was actually happening or the other kept his or her feelings well out of sight or had no way of expressing them short of packing and leaving. Most relationships, however, have plenty of storm warnings when they are about to go on the rocks.

No matter how wonderful it seemed at first, very few long-term or intense relationships are completely free of friction or irritation. Even within a close relationship people are bound to develop and grow as individuals – they may even grow apart – and that process in one partner can sometimes seem to threaten the security of the other. Getting these feelings into some proportion can seem a pretty daunting task.

In the middle of emotional stress or anxiety it is often hard to see clearly what options you have. An unhappy or stressful present can completely blot out the future. There are some obvious decisions you have to make. Perhaps the relationship would work if some changes were made. But even if you and your partner come to terms with difficulties that cannot be changed, thus making you both less unhappy, you may still have to decide whether you would be happier if the relationship ended than you are within it.

You could decide a period apart might help. Perhaps your partner feels the same way or perhaps he or she is unaware of just what is going wrong and would rather put things right than split. You might feel that taking any action at all would provoke just the very disaster you are trying to avoid. Even if you feel that a break-up is unavoidable and that is really what you want, then things you do before it actually happens might make it easier on everyone.

It is very difficult to cope with these problems alone. Talk the problem through with someone – a close friend perhaps, or a trained counsellor. Expert help can be obtained from Relate, a national organisation offering help to anyone with marital problems. There are also religious organisations offering counselling, for example, the Jewish Marriage Council and the Catholic Marriage Advisory Council. Your local Citizens' Advice Bureau will have a list of the addresses of these and any other such organisations in your area.

SEPARATING

If you have made your decision to split, or it has been made for you by your partner, obviously important decisions will have to be made about your future and that of your children. These decisions are not necessarily final, just short-term arrangements.

The matters you will need to discuss on separation include:
- where the children will live and who look after them;
- how you will each support yourselves and the children;
- who will pay outstanding bills, bank card credit repayments and so on;
- who will stay in the house;
- how the rent or mortgage will be paid; what will happen to the joint account if you have one;
- what will happen to the house, car, furniture and other property.

When you separate, the arrangements you make should be fair to both of you. If one partner has been maintained by the other during the marriage, that should continue as far as possible on separation. It makes no difference whose name the home is in. If the home is in one partner's name, he or she cannot simply turn the other partner out. Similarly, the partner who leaves does not lose his or her rights to a share of the home.

If you think your partner may act against your interests, sell property to stop you getting it, or endanger you or your children, get legal advice immediately.

CHILDREN AND THE LAW

Parents who are married to each other share parental responsibility for their children. This will begin when the child is born and continue until the child is 18 years old or marries before that age. This automatic sharing of parental responsibility continues irrespective of whether the parents' marriage breaks down and they divorce.

Parental responsibility means making the major decisions about the child's life; for example, how and where he or she will be educated and in what, if any, religion. The children are better served if both parents continue to be involved in such matters, despite the fact they are no long married. In most cases, since both parents will have their children's welfare at heart, they will agree on such matters, including where the children are to live following divorce and how much contact the children are to have with the parent they do not live with. In these circumstances no court intervention or formal order need be granted. If the parents cannot agree, their solicitors will encourage them to discuss the matter reasonably and to come to an agreement. If this is not possible either parent can apply to court for an order determining the dispute. There is a policy that the court will only intervene in children cases if it is in the child's interest to do so. This means that in most cases following divorce no court order will be made relating to the children and parents will be left to make their own arrangements. In cases where either parents cannot agree or when a dispute arises at a later date, the courts can make one or more of the following orders:

A *residence order* decides where a child is to live and with whom. However, parents remain jointly responsible for all important decisions in the child's life as this order does not alter the fact that they share parental responsibility. It is possible to obtain a split residence order, so the child could live with each parent for stated periods, for example a week or month or a division between school term and holidays.

A *contact order* decides who the child can see, visit or stay with. It can also deal with contact by letter or telephone. Contact orders are usually made in favour of parents to enable outings, visits or weekend stays. However they could be made in favour of any other relation or friend with whom the court feels the child would benefit from seeing or keeping up with.

Most reasonable parents will be able to make their own arrangements about these things, but sometimes residence and contact become a battleground. In Chapter Five you will find some guidelines for dealing with the problems your children will face when you break up. If you can accept these and persuade your partner to accept them, you will most likely be able to sort out the best deal for the children. If you cannot then the court can be asked to decide.

The court can also make two other orders – a *prohibited steps order* and a *specific issue order*. These orders can be used to decide a particular problem, for example education or medical treatment of the child or whether the child should be allowed to emigrate abroad with one of the parents.

You can always go to court if any agreement you make breaks down. The court will not necessarily enforce any prior agreement, but will look at it in relation to the welfare of the children. Even before asking the court to make a decision you can ask for help from a conciliation service. These services exist both within the court system and as independent agencies. Their aim is to help you to reach an agreement about the children without having to resort to a court order. The court will encourage you to try conciliation during court proceedings.

The law does not recognise either parent as having a prior right to have the children living with them on any specific grounds; for example, the age of the children or the sex of the parent. The court will only take into account the welfare of the child in relation to its particular circumstances. In order to achieve some uniformity there is a list of factors that the court must look at, but these just ensure that the court looks at all the circumstances in every case. It is often thought that the mother should be regarded as having a superior right to look after the children. This is not so as a matter of law, but it is true to say that the court will usually consider that the children are better off living with the parent who has been the main giver. If it is the mother then she is more likely to obtain a residence order.

The court will try and establish the children's wishes. Depending on how old and mature they are, the court may take what they want into account when it makes its ruling. The court will usually ask for a report from a court welfare officer which will cover the children's wishes. If necessary medical, psychiatric or psychological reports may also be obtained.

Unlike any other part of the legal process of ending a marriage, in orders for residence or contact the judge may also take into account the behaviour of the parents, but only so as to assess whether he or she is a good parent. For example, the fact that the mother commits adultery is unlikely, in itself, to cause the court to conclude that she is not a good mother. If she is a prostitute, however, the court may question her ability to provide a suitable home for a child.

Normally the court will hear both sides of the argument, but in some emergency cases the court can make an order in the absence of one parent. Such an order, called 'ex parte', is a temporary one and will only last until there can be a full hearing with both parents having their say.

Any order made will last until the child reaches 16. Orders are only made for children over 16 in exceptional circumstances. If one parent does not keep to the order made the other must seek legal advice. The court may order the child to be brought to the applying parent. The defaulting parent can be jailed for persistent breach of an order.

Children may not be taken out of the United Kingdom without the consent of both parents. If a residence order has been made the parent with whom the children live can take them abroad for a holiday not exceeding one month without the consent of the other parent. If you suspect that your ex is about to take the children abroad without your permission you can apply to the court for a prohibited steps order to keep them at home. You can also apply to the police, who in urgent cases can circulate details to the ports and airports to try to stop the children being taken out of the country.

WHO SUPPORTS THE CHILDREN?

Both parents have a duty to provide for their children. From April 1993, maintenance of children will generally be dealt with by the Child Support Agency, who will calculate and enforce payments that parents must make to their children. The maintenance will be assessed according to a formula. The money can be paid either directly to the parent looking after the child or via the Child Support Agency. The courts will no longer be able to make orders in relation to children unless the parents are able to afford more than the Agency assessment, for example, for school fees. Even if the parents agree about the amount of maintenance, the jurisdiction of the Agency cannot be excluded.

The policy used by the agency looks at the income of the support-payer and applies a strict formula to work out how much they can afford to pay. If your partner has simply taken off without trace, you will be entitled to claim welfare benefits for the support of you and your family. In this case steps will probably have to be taken to locate the defaulting parent and force them to meet their obligations to their children.

SPOUSE MAINTENANCE

The mere fact of divorce does not put any automatic responsibility on one partner to provide support for the other, but only where one partner cannot meet his or her reasonable needs. This might be through physical or mental disability or through the inability to get a job that is appropriate or which pays enough.

In most cases one partner is prevented from meeting his or

her reasonable needs by the division of responsibilities decided on within the marriage – one partner chooses to stay at home to look after household and parental obligations while the other goes to work, or one works while the other studies or prepares for some career which will eventually provide support.

After separation one partner might have their previous ability to provide for themselves impaired by some rearrangement of responsibilities. It might be, for instance, that the father gives up his job and stays at home to look after the children while the wife continues her career. In this case the father might be entitled to maintenance from his wife.

During a separation the responsibilities of the marriage continue. If one partner supported the other during the marriage a degree of that support will continue, at least until an alternative agreement is reached. If you cannot agree, again you can apply to court for a maintenance order.

Maintenance may continue after the final dissolution so long as the reasons for it apply – the support and raising of children for instance, inability to earn an income, or a reasonable period for a wife or husband who has supported a partner through education or training to equip themselves for a supportive career.

A maintenance order stops when the person benefiting from it remarries, or when the court orders it to stop on the application of the person paying it, or when both agree to stop payments. It also stops when the maintenance payer dies, unless the maintenance order takes account of this possibility – a matter which should be thought of when the order is being drawn up.

The court will not usually see as relevant a partner's conduct when awarding maintenance unless it is extremely bad misconduct. It will consider only the needs of the partner and the ability of the other to pay. The question of whether one or other has been a 'good' wife or husband will be of no importance.

When setting the amount it will look at each partner's means and their ability to earn, the reasonable needs of the person asking for support, the financial responsibilities of the one who is being asked to pay and the support they are obliged to give others – a new spouse and family perhaps.

The partner paying maintenance will not be obliged to pay an amount that would deprive them of a reasonable standard of living. The law sensibly steps aside from blame or fault and attempts to be fair and reasonable to both parties.

DIVIDING UP THE PROPERTY

Perhaps nothing else has the potential to cause quite so much bitterness and anguish as dividing up the property. Often this has little to do with material values – quite trivial objects which have acquired emotional significance can cause the most astonishing rows. In most cases, neither partner will be better off through the division of their property. In many cases one or both of them will be facing a period of economic hardship worse than they have experienced before.

The old cliché about two people being able to live as cheaply as one acquires a whole new significance when those two break-up. The longer and more established the relationship, the more economic impact it is likely to have.

For that reason, facing this part of the process needs a very clear head. Don't be pressured into making hasty agreements. You may live to bitterly regret them. The more complex the partnership's affairs the more likely it will be that you will need independent and impartial advice. Mediation may be useful. The mediator can help you work out solutions to your disputes. The mediator will see you and your partner without your legal advisers. Details can be obtained from the Citizens' Advice Bureau.

You can, of course, divide up the property in any way you like and it is far better if you and your partner can discuss the matter calmly and reasonably. Remember that if you get into a lengthy legal battle over property, lawyers' costs will mount up quickly and the less there will be to share. You should both be aware, however, that the law takes the view that each of you is entitled to a fair share of the matrimonial property and it is a good idea to get at least some legal advice to ensure that you are not forgoing your legal rights.

If you can agree, a consent order can be drawn up and issued by the court. It can then be enforced and varied by the court. If you can't agree, you will have to ask the court to decide. The two main things the court will consider are the contributions each of you has made to the marriage, and the present and future income, needs and responsibilities of both of you. Contribution does not mean just money. Caring for the home and children is just as important.

The court will often give the parent looking after the

children the greater proportion of the assets. If, as is common, this is the mother, she not only has the expense of rearing the children but usually not as great a capacity as her partner to earn a good income.

Property and maintenance are usually considered together. One spouse may be given a larger share of the assets so that money can be invested to provide an income, instead of being paid ongoing maintenance.

Sometimes establishing your share of the property can be complex and may take some legal untangling. If things are not straightforward, and in most cases even when they are, it is best to get independent legal advice about any agreement. Remember that your partner's solicitor is obliged to work in the best interests of your partner so you should have legal advice of your own.

If you do not have a solicitor and do not know how to go about finding one, then your local citizens' advice bureau or law centre can help you find one. Before you see the solicitor make sure you know exactly what you want to discuss. Even if you already have a solicitor it helps to cut down on expensive interviews if you sort out your needs and questions well in advance. Crying on your solicitor's shoulder can be a very costly indulgence.

WHO GETS TO STAY IN THE FAMILY HOME?

The family home is considered along with all the other matrimonial property and the court has a wide discretion to deal with it. It does not matter whose name the home is in. Both partners have rights in relation to it, regardless of formal legal ownership, in the same way as they have rights to all other family property based on their contribution, both financial and non-financial, to the marriage. The court can order that it be transferred to either the husband or wife, or that it be sold and the proceeds divided or the sale can be postponed until dependent children have grown up.

When there are young children involved, it is often the case that, as there is not enough capital to re-house both parties if the house is sold, the only order that can be made to protect the children's needs for a home is one which delays the sale of the house until they are grown-up.

Along with all other questions on separation and divorce, it is infinitely preferable if the question of the family home can be resolved without the necessity of intervention by the court.

THE LAST ACT

After all you have already been through, the last act might seem something of an anti-climax. There is no high drama involved at the end of the marriage. All the court needs to know is that your marriage has broken down irretrievably and that you can prove one of the five facts. The law will then recognise that your marriage has ended and will issue a decree nisi of divorce which can be made absolute six weeks later. The decree absolute will dissolve the marriage. No decree absolute will be granted unless the court is satisfied that there is no need for any order to be made in relation to the children.

If you want a divorce you will have to start legal proceedings and state on which fact you are relying. If your partner is prepared to agree to the fact the divorce will be undefended, this is known as a 'special procedure' divorce. This type of divorce is granted without any court hearing and neither party need appear at court. The costs of an undefended divorce will be small. If you have very little income and capital you will be entitled to have your solicitor's fees paid by a type of legal aid known as 'Green Form Advice'. If you incur legal expenses for maintenance or children disputes Legal Aid is available, again subject to a means test.

You can marry again as soon as the decree nisi is granted – but read the whole of this book first!

VIOLENCE

Sadly the pain, anger and frustration of a break-up can all too easily spill over into violence. If your partner threatens you with violence or even if you fear they may become violent towards you or your children, then the law can offer you some protection.

Married and unmarried people can get protection from the county courts, which will issue an injunction to your partner not to threaten or assault you or the children (a non-molestation injunction), or to keep away from you and the home (an ouster order). If you are married you can also apply to the Family Proceedings Court for protection.

If it is an emergency and you are being attacked you should call the police. If necessary they can arrest the violent person. Most forces now have specially trained Domestic Violence Units. If you are worried that you might be assaulted on some future occasion, you should seek advice from an advice agency or a solicitor. Legal Aid may be available to cover your costs. The injunction can be tailored to suit your particular circumstances and may prevent your partner entering the place where you live, or hassling you at work or some other place, even if this is in the form of persistent phone calls. If an injunction is disobeyed the offending partner can be arrested and charged and, if convicted, fined or imprisoned. The court can also make orders giving you the right to occupy the family home. With these orders it sometimes is usual to apply for a non-molestation order as well.

If you are threatened with violence, then try to keep your cool and not do anything to make the situation worse. Avoid getting into a slanging match or trading accusations or insults. Get help as soon as you can. If you think that a violent situation might occur, then make sure your friends or neighbours know that you might need help. Even agree on some sort of signal if that might help alert them. Take as many practical steps as you can. The law can give you some help, but it is far from being a real solution to the problem.

WHAT HAPPENS IF YOU WERE NOT MARRIED?

The law is reasonably clear about the rights, obligations and protections it provides for partners in a marriage. It is less clear about couples who have chosen to live together without being married. While the relationship hangs together then the rights and duties expected of each partner are similar to those in a marriage. The mother only automatically obtains parental responsibility for the children. If the father wants to obtain parental responsibility he can do so in a number of ways. If the mother is agreeable they can make a simple agreement to share parental responsibility.

The law about dividing up property, however, is very different. Ideally, partners should draw up a written agreement about what will happen to any property in the event of a bust-up. Such an agreement can be made at any time during the relationship. In the real world very few couples actually do that – not surprisingly, since the rosy glow of passionate courtship is very likely to be chilled by one lover flourishing a draft agreement at the other.

If you have bought a house together for your joint use then the title could be registered in fixed shares, 50/50 or 30/70 or whatever proportions reflect the relative contribution of each partner. If the home is jointly registered in both names then this can be taken to represent an intention to have equal shares. Unlike a marriage, if one partner moves into the home of the other the non-owning partner is not likely to be able to claim a share of the home on break-up, however long the relationship lasted or whatever supported contribution by way of housework or child-minding they had made to the other.

If there is no written agreement and if the home is registered only in one partner's name, then the non-owning partner may only be able to claim a share if he or she can prove that financial contributions were made and what they were.

Alternatively, the couple can make a cohabitation agreement saying how the property is to be divided if the relationship breaks down, and the agreement can be enforced provided they had proper legal advice when it was signed.

The law about the care and maintenance of children will apply equally to married and unmarried parents. The law obliges the father to provide for his child whether or not he is married to the mother. An unmarried custodial parent can apply to the Child Support Agency for child support to be assessed and paid to them in the same way as a married parent.

If the father's name is not on the birth certificate, then the mother may have to apply for a paternity order, unless the father has acknowledged paternity in writing or has otherwise been declared the father. Regardless of the marital state of their parents, all children have the right to inherit from their natural parents and their parents are obliged to support them up until the age of 16.

Only the mother is entitled to make important decisions affecting the child's life unless the father obtains parental responsibility. Then they have equal rights and each or both may apply to the court to resolve any disputes about residence or contact. The court will always decide according to the best interests of the child.

If you agree between yourselves on which parent will have the day-to-day care of the children – and on contact – that is the degree of access to the child the other parent is entitled to have there is no need for any formal agreement to be entered into.

If you can't agree, or if later your agreement breaks down, then you can ask the court to make a decision for you. The court will make a decision based on the welfare needs of your children.

KEEP YOUR COOL

As hard as it might seem the legal aspects of your break-up need to be seen with a clear head and a cool temper. Don't let passion or guilt get in the way of commonsense.

If there are no children and there is no property to speak of, then sometimes the best course is simply to flag the material things away and get your emotional life back in some order again. But, small or large, you are entitled to a fair share of what your relationship accumulated in the way of domestic treasures and don't be talked out of your share.

The best way, of course, is an amicable and reasonable agreement between two adult persons who have decided to go their own way. Sometimes, though, this is just not possible and to unravel the legal and material ties of your marriage or live-together relationship you will need help – advice from a neutral friend or counsellor or legal intervention. Seek help as soon as you strike problems or feel out of your depth.

Looking back now I am amazed at the trivial bits and pieces we chose to have rows about – some silly pot plant became a life and death issue. The big, simple issues, like the house, didn't seem so hard – we could stand back from those I suppose – but the little shared treasures and joys brought back all the pain and guilt in big waves. I envied people who had 'civilised' settlements, although I never actually met any of them. Dividing things up seemed to have an awful finality about it. The emotional ties went first and then the physical symbols of the marriage began to drift away too. I'm glad now that I let time pass before making decisions or agreeing to things. She would get frustrated and angry and her solicitor would get more demanding letter by letter, but standing back from it all was a good thing and it let things go out of my life with a minimum of pain. I had to keep telling myself though, that until we actually got to court, if we were going to end up there, I could take time about things.

He came round one night armed with a bottle of wine and dripping with charm. 'Let's be civilised about this', he said and everything he said seemed so fair and reasonable. Until then I had been too numb to think about what was going to happen on the material side of things. But when I checked it out the next day I realised that this was just another of his charming cons and even a half of the obvious things was a lot more than his 'fair share'.

CHAPTER NINE

Falling in Love Again

I began another relationship almost immediately with a really beautiful person I had fancied for quite some time and who, I discovered, had fancied me. The relationship didn't take away the pain of losing my wife and it didn't muffle the grief, but it was really supportive of my feelings about those things. I felt really confident about starting again. I thought I was sure about what I was and wasn't going to have this time. In fact I wasn't sure about anything at all and now I can see that what I thought was starting again was just cuddling in a great, selfish cocoon. I was too wrapped in myself to hear or feel or see what she might have wanted from our relationship. So it didn't last. Looking back I can't help wishing that I hadn't met her quite so soon; that somebody else not so special had come in between; that I could have been a giver as well as a taker. If there is one thing I would really want to tell people like us it's 'Don't be too quick to start another relationship. Wounded people make lousy lovers. Take your time and become at least mostly whole before you commit another person to your life and you to theirs.'

I wanted so desperately to be 'In Love' again. I didn't want to be single and I didn't want to be independent. I'd spent two years on my own – been there, done that – I wanted the whole environment of being 'In a Relationship'. I found I was off the old social circuit of couples. Women friends would ask me to lunch, but never to dinner. And it seemed impossible to meet men.

. . . .

During the painful process of separation, falling in love again might seem only the most remote possibility. Not only have your self-esteem and your ego take a mighty battering, but the 'once bitten, twice shy' factor will probably make you extremely cautious or fearful when it comes to considering a new relationship. The more you are conscious of your feelings and the more you admit them, then the harder this part of becoming single might seem.

Some newly single plunge immediately into a new affair as a way of numbing or avoiding their feelings about the old. Men are particularly prone to this. Sometimes, of course, a new and successful relationship can begin immediately, but more often than not such instant replacements simply set up a repeat of the last disaster. A lot of unwanted emotional baggage gets carried over from the old to the new and the absent partner can be an ever-present, unwelcome third party in the new relationship.

At the very least it is a good idea to have begun the process of casting off the old before putting on the new. Ideally a new relationship has a better chance of succeeding if you are no longer among the walking wounded and have let go of the old emotional ties.

Even if you have left the relationship to begin another, there will still be a lot of emotional readjusting to do. You may not recognise just how much, but your new partner is likely to find some of it a bit of a strain.

In the process or readjustment – to a new relationship or new singleness – you are almost certain to have discovered your individual self again and, perhaps acquired new emotional skills and a new emotional balance. One bonus of separation is that it can provide you with a whole new view of yourself and a degree of self-reliance which can be an asset in any new relationship.

There is even the possibility that in the process of becoming single you have found a state of mind and a lifestyle that suits you far better than those you had as one half of a couple.

For the first couple of years I really yearned for the security of being a couple – of being in a stable one-on-one relationship. I made all sorts of rash promises to the women I went out with – pledges of undying love that could have been taken as offers of marriage. Thank goodness no-one took me up on any of them because now I have adjusted to being single again and remade my life around that. I am happy that way. Maybe sometime in the future – the distant future – I might take the plunge again, but it would take a pretty extraordinary person to seduce me out of the life I have now.

In the first stages of separation most people find it hard enough to muster sufficient emotional energy to deal with their own immediate problems, let alone enough to project attraction signals to some new person. Don't worry, the condition isn't permanent.

For months after my separation I couldn't bring myself to look at other men. I needed time to recover and friends put lots of pressure on me to go out with new men, but I simply couldn't. I felt too raw and featherless.

Three months after the separation I started spending some time with a woman I'd known for a couple of years. We had some fun together, but I resisted the idea of becoming lovers with her because at the time I felt much too bruised, quite deadened sexually. We talked about it. She was incredibly supportive. After a few more weeks I thought 'Oh hell. Why not?' and despite being a bit scared about it all we began a lovely sexual relationship which did wonderful things for me. In a small way I was reborn. It opened up some parts I thought were dead and helped restore some of my self-confidence which had taken a real battering. I felt much stronger.

Rediscovering your sexuality is often part of the separation process. In the dying stages of the old relationship sex was most likely one of the most obvious casualties. In any case, the sex within a relationship – no matter how sexually adventurous one or both of the partners might be – is likely to have fallen into familiar patterns. But perhaps one of the most pleasant maturities of a long-term relationship is that the hot passions of new-found love evolve into a familiar physical language. Often one of the fears of the newly single is about facing those first passions again.

Attempting to confront that particular fear, or rediscovering a sexual urgency that the dying relationship had buried, can project you into a sometimes damaging excess.

My sex life had been non-existent before my husband left and when he went I really got into it. I found it easy to find sexual partners – for one-night stands anyway. I must have been mad the risks I took. I had to have an abortion and fortunately I got some good, stern counselling about sexual responsibility and proper contraception. But for a while I was in a really self-destructive space – even though I knew the dreadful diseases I might have caught and, worse, spread. But I felt bad so I was bad.

In the swinging seventies and early eighties that kind of response had some dangers, but they probably seemed a reasonably tolerable risk, given the climate of the new sexual revolution. In the AIDS-ridden nineties, looking for Mr Goodbar could be lethal.

Yet sex, stripped from its burden of social and religious customs and prohibitions, is perhaps the most basic of human drives. It carries with it enormous possibilities for solace and pleasure – fleeting as they may be. The contact of flesh against flesh must stir the earliest of memories – warmth, comfort, pleasure and security – an accurate enough list of all the things for which the separated person feels the deepest need.

For a great many, perhaps the majority, of the newly single, sex may seem the most intolerable of deprivations. It may seem all the more so as the other hurts and anxieties begin to heal.

As the hurting dulled and I got back into more ordinary ways of thinking, I began to really ache for sex. I was desperately afraid of it, of the hurt a new encounter might bring, but my body yearned for that warmth of having someone else held close. I had plenty of love and hugs from friends and from the children, but that still left some indefinable thing out — not just simple sexual release but something else I just couldn't explain or talk to anybody about.

I was physically frustrated, but terrified of even getting near raising the subject of sex with any of the women I went out with. I was caught between this panic about being rejected and straight old sexual feelings. Eventually I swallowed my pride, plucked up courage and went to a massage parlour. It was okay I suppose – just marginally better than masturbation – but I was glad I went and found out that it wasn't just sex on its own I was missing. I had pretty mixed feelings after that I can tell you.

I screwed myself silly for months. Anyone, especially those other people's husbands who seemed to be able to read my mind and turned up at the oddest hours with the slimmest excuses. I responded to everyone. I must have been giving out very strong 'fuck me' signals, but I wanted to love everyone and have everyone love me. Sex seemed the quickest way of getting love. It's a common mistake.

For many people a lifetime of particular attitudes towards sex can be an insurmountable barrier or, depending on your point of view, a protective shield. Many women and a reasonable number of men have been culturally conditioned not to seek casual, recreational sex.

If you have been comfortable with that view, then separation should not necessarily provide an influence to change that. There is sometimes a danger though that the combination of such attitudes with a perfectly normal physical need might lead to quite trivial emotions being unduly inflated. To overcome moral prohibitions some newly single women and men are tempted to convince themselves they have 'fallen in love', further confusing their emotional systems and, perhaps, setting up a new trigger for hurt and guilt.

It was probably my upbringing, but I could no more have slept with another man after we split than flown. Once the divorce was complete I was able to start out and look for a lover and companion. I didn't want choice or experimentation.

Whatever the physical urgency or otherwise of your sexual needs, this is one part of your life you could truly regard as a minefield. Putting aside moral considerations – and they will play whatever role you choose – an incautious, headlong plunge into new sexual encounters can do you a great deal of harm – physically and emotionally.

One thing you should ignore, though, is a fear of being hurt. Perhaps you will and perhaps you won't, but pain is the risk currency of emotional transactions and if you are not prepared to invest some, you may find satisfying relationships remain elusive.

The most immediate potential for emotional harm is adding to your current burden of guilt. Your susceptibility to this will depend, to a large extent, on a whole range of moral and emotional prohibitions you will have built up within your relationship. Most relationships – with allowances for a small degree of slippage here and there – are based on a one-to-one sexual commitment. To dump that casually may not be easy, or at least as easy as the heat of a sexual moment might make it seem.

The dangers of physical harm we come to later.

Take some time to stand back from your body and make some careful choices about how you want to deal with this part of its needs. Take some advice if you have any doubts. Talk to friends who may have gone through the same stage as you, or seek some counselling.

It is important too, not to be pressured into sex if you don't want it, out of any fear of losing a new relationship or to prove some point to yourself or your defecting partner.

Most marriage guidance councils offer relationship counselling for individuals or pre-marriage and re-marriage courses, which can be of help. When looking for advice, just keep in mind the need to avoid someone using your vulnerability to impose their moral views, prejudices or stereotypes on you. Perhaps the best rule of thumb is not to run against the grain of your own feelings, moral, emotional and physical. They may be in conflict, so decide on which seems to feel best having priority. What you are considering is the most personal of choices and the decision has to be yours, based on your needs and feelings.

When I visited my GP for a pap smear and check up he made me feel terrible. I'd been separated for two years and had had three sexual partners. He said I was promiscuous. That's what they call women who have had three or more partners. What would he have called my ex, who must have slept with a hundred women? Attaboy, probably.

I know it seems a dumb thing for a bloke to worry about, but I did worry about sleeping with a lot of different women. Not really moral worries or disease ones – I was careful about that – but just a nagging doubt that beyond the immediate pleasures I wasn't doing myself, or them, a whole lot of good. My real problem was, who to talk to? My doctor, with sly grins, gave me a quick catalogue of sexually transmitted diseases with a sort of 'go for it' overtone. I didn't have to try discussing it with other blokes – I knew the nudge, nudge stuff that would provoke. In the end I talked to a woman friend, who had been close in and out of the marriage. She was really good – not judgemental as I expected a woman to be. She encouraged me to get a better view of the whole thing, to sort of get in touch with how I actually felt. It turned out to be good old-fashioned guilt, which I did not need. Did I mend my ways? Well that's another story.

A friend laughingly gave me a vibrator when my husband left, with the advice that it was better and safer to masturbate than have meaningless sexual encounters. She was right. I was hopeless for well over a year, trying to make love. I took a long time to let go of my anger and hatred for my ex. I met some lovely men too, but I was nowhere near ready to be loving and giving.

Possibly another generation or more might have to pass before we will know whether the current fears about the scale of the

AIDS epidemic are justified. In the meantime it is foolish to ignore what seem to be very real risks. However, the basic advice to stick to only one sexual partner for life, is likely to have a hollow ring for someone who has just left such a relationship and is not particularly drawn to a life of solitary celibacy.

The AIDS virus is transmitted by the exchange of body fluids – semen or blood, or fluids which contain either of those. Obviously the most common occasion for such an exchange is during sexual intercourse. The most immediate line of defence is a condom. If you have never used one before, now is the time to start. Short of staying celibate there is no other effective protection.

The disease can be transmitted from men to women and women to men. The responsibility for protection must be your own – male or female, make sure that if you are about to have sex with a new partner use a condom – if you or they don't have one, don't make love. It simply is not worth the risk. There is no cure for AIDS, no vaccine against it and no second chances.

It can be transmitted by people who have no obvious symptoms and who may not even know they have been infected.

Before embarking on any new physical relationship it would make some sense to know as much as you can find out about your prospective partner's sexual history. There are a number of groups particularly at risk – homosexual or bisexual men and intravenous drug takers are the most obvious. The virus can be transmitted by needle-sharing as well as sexual intercourse.

Just statistically, people who have had a large number of sexual partners might also be at risk. If they have lived or travelled to some of the cities where AIDS has reached epidemic proportions that risk might be larger.

This is one area of finding out about a new partner where delicacy or timidity could be a fatal flaw. On the other hand, use some commonsense and do not unnecessarily interrogate a prospective good new relationship out of existence. But just keep in mind that you are making decisions about your body and your health.

To bring the subject up, I say, 'There are three things I hate: cold toast, waiting in queues, and social diseases.' It always raises a laugh and an invitation to talk about our sexual history. I always carry condoms. And I always bring up the subject before one item of clothing has been removed and the kisses get too hot.

AIDS is, of course, not the only sexually transmitted disease you should be cautious about. There is a whole range of others with effects ranging from the drastic to the uncomfortable. A refresher course is a sensible precaution if you are beginning single life again and see new sexual relationships as being a part of your new life.

Your doctor can give you plenty of advice, but just make it clear it is advice you want and not some moralistic lecture if you have a GP given to that kind of attitude. A citizens' advice bureau, marriage guidance council or local hospital clinic, usually the most anonymous source you could go to, could also supply you with information on sexually transmitted diseases.

On top of the basic drive to sex, there can be other, more subtle motivations towards new physical relationships. Not the least of these is a kind of yearning for revenge on the other partner. They have rejected you, so you will show them you can hack it in the real world by sleeping with everyone in sight.

For a large number of men and more than a few women, this urge can be manifested in an obsessive attraction to younger partners. It feeds the ego and it sends out punishing messages to the ex partner. There is, of course, nothing inherently wrong with beginning again with someone younger. Obviously a majority of single and available people are going to be in younger age groups, but there are traps for new players here too.

Cruelly, the world and its dog take relationships between older men and younger women mostly in their stride; the other way about is a very different matter. Older women and younger men are likely to be the butt of cruel and callous jokes and subjects for humiliation and scorn. There is no rational reason for this and if you can weather what comes your way, then other people's prejudice is no reason for making alterations to your emotional life.

I was 44 and he was half that. It was a lovely relationship in every way, but for some reason I found hard to explain it made me feel socially very uneasy. We seldom went out anywhere together in public – my choice not his – and when we did take a holiday together we went overseas. I eventually couldn't stand the strain any more and I ended it. I wish now I had had more courage about society and more confidence that it would have worked.

For men, oddly enough, the envy of married male acquaintances can be something of a burden. It can even degrade the relationship by offering the temptation to adopt the macho, bit-of-an-old-dog attitudes their male friends attribute to it. Young women need this like a hole in the head.

I took a new girlfriend to a restaurant party, a celebration of Bastille Day. She was very much younger than me. We had only been out a couple of times before – we certainly were not yet lovers. I was amazed and embarrassed at the way my male friends behaved to her. They seemed to think she was an easy lay or something equally crude. They gave her a hard time and kept referring to me as 'Grandad'. Eventually I blew up and told them exactly what I thought of them. I didn't pull any punches, although it would have been easier just to go along with it. I told them exactly what they were doing. I pointed out how I thought their wives, who were there, must feel. To their credit they were mostly ashamed and I realised that their behaviour was more thoughtless than intentionally rude. It did teach me what to expect though. The good thing was that it deepened the relationship. We had a taste of the problems, we shared them and ended up with a lot of respect for each other. We became lovers that night – the beginning of a good and sensitive relationship that lasted quite a while and still survives as a good supportive friendship.

Relationships of this kind can involve a kind of culture shock. Married and single are two quite different cultural environments in the broadest sense of that word. That difference tends to be deepened when there is also a difference in generations. It is more than just a difference in tastes. For the older partner there is likely to be a whole new set of attitudes and behaviours to come to terms with, some of them challenging and stimulating, some daunting.

Living in a big city it is easy to get isolated in a kind of married village. Your circle is pretty restricted and after you have busted up meeting someone new is a real problem. I found that the people I met were all heaps younger than me — there were not a lot of single forty-year-old women around the clubs and places I acquired a taste for. Actually I found it pretty exciting learning about a whole lot of new tastes and styles I had paid no attention to before. It was a bit like being launched into an entirely new world — like old Rip van Winkle waking up. I didn't try to be younger — I just accepted where I was and the people I was with and they accepted me for the most part.

Meeting new people can seem a formidable task if you have been out of circulation for any length of time. The situation will not be helped by the state of your ego at the beginning of your separation.

To a large extent, your courage about getting back into the world will have a great deal to do with forming new friendships and relationships. If you lurk about in your own protected nest, nursing your misery, you may be there in that state for some time. Work on keeping the friendships you already have intact and accept any opportunity that gives you to make new ones or meet new people.

Accepting dinner and party invitations can seem more than a little bit frightening if you are used to going to such things as a couple. Be courageous and go. You can always leave if it gets too much to handle.

Night classes, hobby clubs, church groups and volunteer organisations are one good way of meeting new people. There are some clubs and social groups particularly designed to bring single people together. The public notices column in your local newspaper may advertise some of these or a citizens' advice bureau might help you locate one.

If you are particularly courageous and social, singles bars and nightclubs can provide stimulating company. It might be company looking for something a little less than a meaningful relationship, however, so use some commonsense if you are going to launch yourself back into this very assertive singles scene.

Check your local newspaper's personal column. This can be a very useful way of meeting people in the same situation as yourself. Treat some of the credentials offered with a reasonable degree of scepticism – these are advertisements after all – and be prepared for a few disappointments. That financially secure young businessman might be none of those things, and that lively, attractive young woman might be similarly short of the mark.

Answer and advertise with caution. Avoid giving too many personal details like telephone number or home address at the outset. Arrange your first meeting in some neutral place – a café would do. It is far better to take a little time over the meeting than lumber yourself with a pest or pervert you can't get rid of short of changing your address or telephone number.

Be certain about just what kind of person you are trying to

meet. Design your advertisement to be as specific as possible. Look at the advertisements that would attract you and the ones that you think might be from people who are like yourself.

I tried a computer dating service to meet new men. It was a strange feeling, like looking for a good second-hand car! But I lived on the outskirts of a newish town, had no car, few friends and very little money. I got plenty of replies. The good thing was being able to be very honest if you didn't think it was worth pursuing a relationship. I met a couple of nice guys.

When we were married my wife and I used to sit in bed on a Saturday morning having a good old laugh at the ads in the personal column. After the split they didn't seem so funny any more – a lot of them sounded like how I felt. Half for a date and half seriously I put in an ad. I got a lot of replies – most obviously hopeless, but I met a couple of nice women and had a pleasant time with them. Neither came to anything more, but it did a lot to help me know I wasn't completely washed up.

Like everything else in the process of becoming single, falling in love again – or even making a happy choice not to – will happen in its own season. It is not a part of your regrowth that you should panic about or rush headlong into the first opportunity that offers.

New relationships will be as deep and satisfying as you are able to make them. If you are still staggering about in shock or nursing a severely wounded ego you are not really likely to make any sensible decisions about something new. When you feel good about yourself you will have a much clearer view of how you can successfully relate to other people.

I spent a lot of time agonising about me being with somebody again. I didn't spend too much time on who or why or what I was going to be. Of course it didn't happen. It didn't happen until I had put in a lot of work on myself and my own life. I think I thought I would just be swept up and carried away by somebody who would nurse away the hurts and blot out the ex. Who needs that? Real people want to get and to give love to real people, not hand out first aid and massages to the injured, and I don't blame them – I don't want that myself.

CHAPTER TEN

What Will You Do This Time Tomorrow?

I remember looking at the keys in my hand. They were all mine. My front door, my car, my life. Even though I was relieved that the marriage was over, the agony and indecision of the last year had taken its toll. I felt if I wasn't careful I would sink out of sight. I spent the whole weekend, mostly in bed, making huge lists. I started with trying to remember what I wanted when I first left home, what I wanted from life, and marriage (at least I could still laugh). Then I started to plan bright spots for the near future – a weekend away, planning a new garden, night classes, joining a singing group, all the things I could think of. The kids did theirs too and we spent a lot of time going over how life would be the same and how it would be different.

I was so numb that it was a long time before I could think ahead through a whole day, let alone consider the day after. But I remember when that suddenly changed. I used to spend a lot of time window-shopping and one day I saw a duvet in a linen shop sale – they weren't too common then. I had slept in them in Germany and always wanted one, but my wife thought they were too hot in the summer so it was just another of those put-aside things. I bought this one anyway and carried it home sort of furtively. When I woke up under it the next morning I felt like that Greek philosopher in his bath – suddenly a last bit of the puzzle had fallen into place, I could do what I liked!

. . . .

After the turbulence of separation, a state of inertia is a fairly usual condition. Not thinking, not agonising and not planning the next immediate step will seem like a welcome period of calm. So it is. Indulge yourself in it, but not for too long. Too much of this good thing can soon become a chronic state of numbness in which nothing seems possible and nothing can be achieved. Planning for the future is a marvellous therapy. However you arrived there, breaking up is a new beginning. Make the most of it.

If you are still living in the place you once shared with your ex-partner, change might seem difficult. You will be surprised to discover how wrong you are and how some quite simple decisions about your living space – focussed on yourself – can seem like a radical breakthrough. Even something as basic as shifting the living room furniture around.

There are two areas of change over which you have some immediate control: your surroundings, to make them closer to how you want them to be; and your personal growth – learning new skills, meeting new people and trying new ways to organise your life.

Making lists is one good way of bringing these things out into view. As one half of a couple, most of the things you have done almost certainly had some element of compromise. Very few couples are perfectly compatible. They reach that pleasant state by balancing one set of expectations against another.

Small or large, there are bound to be some things in your immediate environment that you would have liked to be another way. Perhaps there are ambitions and goals you put aside for one reason or another. These might be as small as an evening hobby class or a trip to some intriguing country town, or as large as a university degree or a walk in the Hindu Kush.

One of my first reactions was to make a bitter sort of catalogue of all the things I hadn't done because she didn't approve or want to. I felt that large chunks of ambition had been censored out of my life. The truth was that most of those things were out of reach anyway and I was just assigning blame where it didn't belong. Everybody told me to be more positive about our split, so I made a list of some of those things I could do now if I wanted to – mostly pretty trivial, but a few that really would make big changes in my life.

Start with your house or flat. If the whole thing seems too large to tackle, then begin with the room you use the most or the room where you do most of your thinking. Write down what you like and what you don't. Then make a plan – this bit today, that bit tomorrow, this other bit when you have saved up enough.

If dumping some unloved or unlovely thing or piece of furniture figures on your list, then throw it out ruthlessly – you may even have enough of these for a garage sale. Culling your unwanted domestic possessions can be a great stimulus for thinking positively about the future. You might do the same thing with your clothes.

During the decline of our marriage our house had taken on a really unloved feel. The bathroom was half painted and the path needed paving out to the clothes line. Dozens of small things I could have quite easily done myself or got someone in to do, but I looked on them as proof of his loss of love for me. About a month after he had gone I got a terrific feeling of energy and started to do the jobs I could do. I ripped off all the crappy wallpaper I had hated for years. I fell in love with my house.

Our living room was a real no man's land – the one part of the house where we could never agree. It was not that we ever argued about it, but it just wouldn't ever turn into a part of our life. About a year after we split I decided I'd had enough of the room as it was and as an anniversary present to myself I made it into the kind of room I had always wanted – the result was bloody marvellous and getting there so simple that I wondered why we hadn't been able to make it work in the 18 years we had lived together in the house. When my ex-wife saw it she burst into tears – she had left and I think she saw the new room as a kind of final symbol of that. It was a symbol for me too – a proof that my life could be different and better than before.

When I first started to do up my new house I found it almost impossible to make up my mind about anything. I was so used to referring everything to him that I felt powerless to decide on my own. I soon got the hang of it though and realised that if I did make a mistake he wasn't around to pounce on that either and what I had done I could just as easily undo – it was a wonderful challenge and it made a lot of changes in the way I approached other things about my life too.

Even if you have to move out of your home and to a new neighbourhood the same kind of process will apply. Make a kind of shopping list of the things you want in your new environment. Obviously your economic situation will determine a lot, but you can at least avoid the obvious mistakes.

Light and sunshine are very important when you will need all the cheerfulness you can muster. So will accessible services if you are at home all day, or most of the day, with children. Shops, bus stops, schools and parks should be reasonably near by. As obvious as these things might seem, they still need to be planned for.

There is always a temptation to try to repeat the previous environment when flat or house hunting. Consider what changes you might like so that even if your move is downwards in economic terms it might still be a great leap forward in terms of improving your lifestyle.

Clinging to a familiar environment can seem comforting, but that old space carries with it all kinds of hidden messages – ghosts of the past relationship. Even if the changes you can make are small, or if a new home has to be chosen on purely economic grounds, be sure to relate change or choice to something you want. As much as you can, make your choices a reflection of yourself, your own needs and personality.

I couldn't help thinking that living alone was a bit like that story about the dog with two bowls of food and starving because he couldn't choose one or the other. The agony of making choices. It seemed so hard. Everything and nothing seemed possible. I just wasn't used to thinking of myself and not running it past his approval in my mind.

As you begin to feel more sure of yourself and more certain in your new status, deciding to move may begin to seem a good idea. Suburbs tend to emphasise family life and if you are alone you may feel that kind of environment jars. A change of scale might be appropriate. Moving from a house to a compact apartment, for instance, may give you a greater sense of control over your domestic affairs.

Your changed relationship might also mean that you can locate yourself in a more convenient address – closer to work for instance, or nearer to the things you like to do in your leisure time. You may even want to be closer to the kind of street life and energy that city living offers.

Whatever you choose, just keep in mind that a move should always be towards something better and not just a negative response to loss. A change of location just for the sake of change does not always solve problems.

Moving to another city with my job a year after separating has been a very important change. Frankly I welcomed the chance to get out of my home town's social goldfish bowl where I was constantly running into her with her new man. In a new city with only a small number of friends I've really put myself on the line and made some important personal decisions about what sort of person I am, what sort of people my friends are, where I live, with whom. The negative aspects are the loss of regular contact with old friends and with my kids, although I still see a lot of them. Sometimes I get attacks of the horrors and wonder whether I've done the right thing. But it has also been a constructive time in which to grow in my own way, standing on my own feet, exploring new relationships, which has sometimes been very exciting.

Selling and dismantling a long-established household can be an exhaustive and expensive business. And you may not just be quitting a neighbourhood – you may also be unplugging from an important and supportive social network that you have taken for granted. Being recognised and indulged by the local grocer or butcher can often be a significant ingredient in your self-esteem.

We live a lot of our our ordinary lives on autopilot and physical familiarity plays a strong role in that. On the other hand having to focus sharply on ordinary things can stimulate a whole range of positive responses about other things in your life.

Some separated people caution that deciding to move should not be considered 'until four seasons have passed'. In any case it is prudent to wait until the dust has settled and give yourself plenty of time to weigh up the pros and cons.

Sometimes a temporary move can help you make up your mind. House or flat swapping with friends is one good way to test the benefits of change.

I hated the suburbs. I had never been particularly fond of living in the quarter-acre paradise, but as a man newly singled it was just too much – a sort of concrete recrimination, a place purpose-built for families which I no longer was. It took me a long time to wrench myself free from a house I sweated blood to pay for and make the way it was, but I knew it no longer was the right kind of place to live. I had a vague idea of what I wanted and until that idea took some real shape I just flailed about. When I finally worked out exactly what I wanted, it turned up and after I had moved in I never gave the old place another thought.

Perhaps even more important than changing the look or feel of your physical surroundings are the changes you can make to the patterns and processes of your domestic life. You may still be a parent, but you are no longer a partner. Eating habits and housekeeping patterns can change to be the way you want and need them.

The old familiar ways may have suited your life as a couple, but your life has changed and so should some of the ways you live it. Following the old routines can provoke painful reminders of an empty space beside you in the car, at the table, in the bed. Change the patterns and leave no room for those spaces.

It took us a while to realise all the restrictions that were off. The dog could sleep on my bed. The kids could be knee deep in Lego in their room. We could eat Chinese food three times a week if we wanted to. God did not strike us dead if we forgot to put the milk bottles out. I didn't have to be a housewife any more. We all mucked in. The house wasn't as spotless as before, but we chugged along with no outbreaks of cholera or visitations from above.

A whole lot of pressures went when she left. It wasn't that she was a nag or anything, but there was always a sort of unspoken expectation about things like cutting the lawn or doing those odd fix-it-up jobs that seemed designed to fill up the weekend. She had so much physical energy and didn't care for things like reading or just thinking. Now I fit the lawns in to my moods not hers and jobs get done when I feel motivated. It's a lot more fun that way and in a funny way involves a lot more pride too somehow. Things seem to get done quicker and more efficiently when you actually choose to do them.

Don't look at the new chores you might have to do with resignation or bitterness. Make a positive decision to learn how to accomplish new skills and add to your sense of independence. While women might take delight in not ironing pyjamas or shirts, men might find the new skill of ironing a great pleasure.

I reverted back to proper cotton shirts after years of drip-dry nylon. I really enjoyed wearing crisp cotton. I resurrected some beautiful old cotton sheets too. Delicious sleeping in cool cotton. I could hear my ex-wife's voice, 'Too much bloody bother bleaching and ironing. Blah blah blah'.

Even in relationships where domestic jobs are shared and not stereotyped there are skills which will tend to fall towards one partner or the other. It can be a liberating experience for a woman to discover that the interior of a car bonnet is not an arcane mystery only men can unravel, or for a man to find that male-kneaded dough can also rise into delicious bread.

Learning new skills can generate a great deal of self-esteem.

Going to classes can also provide opportunities for meeting new people. Your local school, polytech, library or citizens' advice bureau will hold lists of what adult classes are available in your area. You may be surprised at their range.

I had always felt intellectually inferior to my husband. I don't think it was anything that he did particularly, it was just that I was the home person and he went out every day to do battle with figures and ideas and negotiations and that kind of thing. A friend was going to night classes, doing Italian and she persuaded me to go with her. That was two years ago. Now my Italian is pretty good — it seems I had a flair for languages that I would never have uncovered if I was still married. I'm planning to go to Italy soon — and on my own!

I thought I'd buy a microwave to make cooking things easier. Not that I had the faintest idea about cooking — I suppose I thought it would be good for heating things up or defrosting frozen dinners — that sort of thing. The shop was throwing four cookery lessons in as a deal. I thought, 'What the hell. Might as well give it a go.' Now I'm a passable cook, but the real point was that I met this really neat woman there and through her a whole lot of other new people.

If classes do not suit you then volunteer or community groups might. You may not be exactly up to fielding calls for Lifeline or the Samaritans, but getting involved with other people in a supportive way can be very rewarding.

One miserable day I met an old lady who was out walking — very shakily too — from her old people's retirement home. She became a very good friend, and I visited her regularly. She was separated from the rest of the world by age. It made my separation from my piggy husband seem a very small thing. I loved being considered a 'young thing' by all the oldies there. I was fifty-two!

Now that you have reached a stage in the process of becoming single when the future seems at last to hold some promise, it is a good time to take stock of your emotional progress. Make a list of your achievements to date. Don't bother with the negative side of this balance sheet, just count up the positive things you have done.

Give yourself credit for the progress you have made. Think back to the time when all you could think about was 'poor, poor, pitiful Me'; when your house seemed like a tomb for a dead relationship and the future seemed full of dreary nothingness.

Some of your past sadness and pain might seem laughable to you now, but it was real then and it is something you have battled through. Feel good about yourself and and treat the new you to some small celebration – or even a large one if you can afford to.

In the back of my wardrobe I put up a calendar and every night I'd tick off how many times I had thought about my ex. Some days were thick with crosses and others had only one or two. After about three months I only looked at it once a week. I kept a very full diary too, having never thought about 'feelings' much before. Now I wanted to write about them. I wasn't very good at talking to friends and I only had one who was also separated, but she was well over the worst. It felt good checking on my progress this way — especially on low days when I felt I was back to square one I could see that bad days pass and get fewer all the time.

The best reaction I had was from an old friend when she saw me after a gap of a few months. Her jaw dropped and she said she couldn't believe the difference in me and how wonderful I was looking. Her response was so genuine I really glowed for ages. I shouted myself a bunch of violets on the way home.

The feeling that you have finally made it through all the misery is pretty good, but even more satisfying is the thought that you actually achieved something positive on the way. I look around my flat now, at the different way I dress, I think about new friends and the new relationship I have with some of the old ones and I let myself feel a bit smug. When you start out you know things are going to be different, but you never realise that they just might be better too.

The return of optimism is a real cause for celebration. No other single feeling is a better gauge of your recovery. For weeks, months or even for years the future has seemed bleak and empty. Then one day it has filled up again with dreams, plans and ambitions. They might be modest or they might be crazy castles in Spain, but they are there and they are yours.

I can't say exactly when it happened, but there was a sort of crossover point. One day I was groping through some miserable fog and the next I was day-dreaming about what I was going to do next year — a holiday I thought I'd have, the kind of house I wanted to live in. None of these schemes was grandiose and some I knew I probably couldn't afford, but the important thing was I didn't have to censor or discard them for any reasons other than my own. That quote about being 'master of my destiny and captain of my fate' kept popping into my mind.

CHAPTER ELEVEN

The Separated Man

I was at dinner one night with a man I didn't know too well. It was a business thing. I was rabbiting on as usual about my life and hard times and I thought I was really being a bit selfish – or worse, boring – so to change tack a bit I asked him about his wife. He didn't say anything much – a sort of conversational shrug – so I went back to me and then I noticed a tear drip off his nose and on to his plate and I thought, 'Oh Christ, another one of us'. And he was. He and his wife had just split. And I thought, 'Well at least you can cry. That's a bloody good start', and I thought about how hard it had been for me to talk to other blokes about how I really felt. Always coming up against the usual macho bravado and innuendo. So I convinced him that I genuinely envied him his tears and I got him to talk. I don't know whether either of us made much sense, but it felt pretty good to share a common experience – sharing it with women friends, which I could do quite easily, was sort of abstract by comparison.

Although I had a good marriage, or it seemed good to me, I often used to fantasise about not being married and about what I would do with that dubious freedom. Somehow I would always pull back, though, from counting the losses that would also involve. I must have been avoiding my worst fears, because when it happened for real I felt I'd been run over by a Mack truck. I felt so ashamed, like I was guilty of something or failed at some important test. I couldn't tell any of my friends or anyone at work. I just let it eat me up from the inside. If the truth were known I suppose my pride was as badly hurt as my heart. I spent a lot of time ignoring the reality and pretending it was a temporary thing.

. . . .

Most men are poorly equipped to cope with emotional trauma. Their schooling, sports and work environments tend to emphasise male values which have little to do with the easy expression of emotional pain or fears. The majority of males grow up never questioning the cliché that boys don't cry, or the stereotypes that allow emotional licence to women and demand staunchness and stoicism of men.

The popular male models in literature, sport and film are not given to tears. Their response to adversity is physical action and exaggerated displays of courage. They do not show disappointment or defeat. Men who run against this particular social grain are depicted as objects of scorn – craven losers or cowards who deserve no sympathy. Men in more serious literature or films can occasionally break this mould but, in the main, male role models eschew displays of emotion.

The stereotype is a cruel one. It is a model which demands that men suspend what are natural human responses in favour of acting out false behaviours, simply to earn social approval.

The potential for dangerous stress in this is immense – particularly where men's normal lives do not bear much resemblance to the male models they are expected to emulate. It is little wonder that increasing numbers crack under the strain of being normal feeling creatures, when they are expected to be Rambo, and adopt a Rambo reality with lethal effect.

Beyond the pains of grief and loss of love the emotional storms of separation carry with them other elements which men find particularly hard to cope with or express. The more men have adopted macho stereotypes the more likely they are to see separation as a violation of their masculinity and the taking away of love as the theft of something to which they had an inalienable right. Wounds of pride and ego cut deep in men, perhaps deeper than they do in women.

When she told me it was finished and that she was not coming back, I simply refused to accept it. I told her she had No Right and other similarly pompous things. I demanded that she come back, that she see sense and so on. I even threatened her with parental authority – how my parents would despise her and how her parents would give her no support for walking out on her commitment. It never occurred to me then that my wrath wasn't righteous. In fact it took a few unsuccessful attempts to install someone as a replacement before I began to realise that things weren't as I saw them at all; that the real world and real relationships did not function like that – like some bloody unbreakable contract where things were owed and, no matter what, you paid up.

The first few weeks were okay. I could see that the marriage had finished. I didn't want to, but going on with it was obviously out of the question. I set out to be reasonable, to be civilised about things like the house and other property we had to divide. Then, through a chance comment by a friend at a party, I discovered that she had taken up with this other guy. That finished my reasonableness – I was in a blind rage. I called her everything I could think of and accused her of all kinds of things. I felt betrayed – so badly betrayed that anything I did to punish her was justified. Yet what had changed? The marriage had finished just the same, whatever the cause. The difference was that now my pride was gone too.

Men find it very hard to come to terms with the fact that their partner has ceased to love them and now loves somebody else. It is a matter of pride and ego, but that does not make it any less painful or stressful – it also has a great deal to do with social conditioning. As unjustified as they are, old social attitudes about the role of women die hard. In the stress of separation men will often seize on those outmoded and unfair conventions to justify their anger and to apportion blame.

Many men also have the added problem of living at something of a distance from their relationships. If the relationship is the traditional one of working husband and homekeeping and mothering wife, the male is often unlikely to be as aware of the deterioration of the relationship. He may well use his working time separation as a shield from the reality and will retreat into work as an escape from emotional difficulties or use it as an excuse for not confronting problems in the relationship.

Men also lack the same kind of emotional support structures that women have traditionally had. They are less likely to talk freely to other men about their emotional life or their relationship, particularly if they are uneasy about those things. They are more inclined to put on what they consider is a brave front and dismiss real problems, to which they contribute, as some temporary thing mainly imagined by their partner.

As a result of this social conditioning about the respective roles of men and women in relationships and their emotional inhibitions, for many men separation can arrive as a chilling bolt out of the blue. They have ignored or hidden from the storm warnings. They do not naturally think of their female partner as initiating major changes in the relationship. When the break-up finally happens they are totally unprepared for it.

The first reaction for many men is an exaggerated form of the SHOCK/DENIAL phase of the grief process. They simply refuse to admit what is happening. The immediate trauma is driven deep out of sight – often buried under rage and recriminations or a desperate plunge into workaholism. Not only do men tend to conceal the reality of the separation from themselves, but they will go to great lengths to hide it from friends or colleagues at work.

In this condition men become prime candidates for anti-social behaviours – excessive drinking for instance – and stress-related physical or emotional crack-ups. Most dangerously of all, they can often turn their anger and pain into increasingly aggressive behaviour towards their ex-partner. Men's violence in separation is a major social problem, so much so that legal sanctions such as non-violence or non-molestation orders have to be enforced in an attempt to limit their potential for damage. Sadly, such orders have little effect on men who have simply lost control of their anger and are beyond the reach of reason or sanction.

Such angry behaviour is a dangerous mixture of a desire to punish for inflicted hurts and an attempt to force the weaker partner back into the relationship. It is a bizarre paradox, but many men believe that they can force someone to love or live with them again, by threatening or abusing them physically.

Men who feel their anger getting out of control or who realise that anger has been a negative part in their relationship should seek help immediately. They may choose to consult an individual counsellor or take part in a men's group or anger management course. A citizens' advice bureau or marriage guidance council will have information about these. The first steps they should take, however, should be to face the reality of the separation, to express their emotion and, perhaps hardest of all for some men, swallow their pride and see what is happening to them as no vast reflection on their manhood, but something quite normal, carrying no great burden of blame or guilt.

I spent a lot of energy and time feeding my anger and almost none coming to grips with the real problems I had. I would get into blind rages and ring her up at all hours, cajoling and threatening. I would turn up at our old home to catch her out and do the same at the insurance office where she had got a job. If social functions brought us anywhere near each other I would either storm out or make some nasty scene. She took out a non-molestation order and even that didn't stop my self-righteous, or so I thought, recriminations. A few run-ins with the police sobered me up a bit, but I didn't really get the message until one thoughtful – and very large – cop convinced me it was just not on and I needed help before I went inside for a stretch. God, I'd hardly had more than a parking ticket and here I was looking at jail. Marriage guidance put me on to an anger management group and that helped a lot.

Shortly after the bust-up a male friend who was still married – quite happily as I thought at the time – gave me some very good advice. He said 'Accept that the separation is forever, don't hold on to false hopes, and sell the house.' He was right, and although it did nothing to soften the blow accepting that we were not going to get together again ever, at least it gave me a positive point to start from. So did selling the house. The irony was that when his marriage came apart a few years later I was able to give his advice back to him. He didn't accept it and had a rough ride for a start.

Half a dozen of us formed a men's group which met every fortnight. Two of us were recently separated and a third fell out of an affair while the group was running. The objective was to analyse sexism both in ourselves and society. But simply in meeting regularly we built up a marvellous closeness, which I really came to treasure. I looked forward to the fortnightly meetings and gained a lot from sharing experiences. I was able to analyse what had gone wrong in my marriage and try to figure out what lessons I could learn from this, in particular things to do with being a male. As a result of these meetings I think I understand a little better now what really happened in the last year or two of the marriage.

To cope with the trauma of separation and to transform it from negative pain into a positive opportunity the separated man has to learn how to talk about and confront his emotions. There is no shame involved in tears and regrets. Admitting to the reality of separation is not going to have some lethal effect on the male genitals.

The separated man may avoid the immediate stress-related results of hiding from the reality of the break-up by burying his pain and loss in another relationship. Such arrangements made in haste may succeed and form the basis of a successful and happy partnership, but more often than not they merely set up a repeat of what has happened before.

Unless the separated man can learn the real nature of the break-up and understand what went wrong, what did not work and what his contribution to all that was, then he is likely to become an emotional time bomb waiting to destroy yet another loving encounter.

It was great at first and I had the extra pleasure of giving my ex no satisfaction thinking that I was doing without the comforts of kitchen and bed. Then the gloss began to wear off and I realised I knew nothing at all about this new woman and that this new happy-ever-after love affair was going to be even shorter-lived than the last. We began to row and I heard myself repeating the same old accusations and silly gibes I had shouted at my ex. Dumb stuff, like running on the spot. I had got nowhere and wasn't going to get anywhere. How miserably true is that saying that those who don't learn from history will go on repeating it.

I had plenty of opportunity to fall in love again – or at least to fall in lust

– but something, it may have been the old notion of once burnt, twice shy, or just emotional laziness, kept me at arm's length from another relationship. As a result I found out some quite surprising things about myself. I actually liked being alone. I didn't become a monk or anything like that, but I valued my own space and my own control over things, even domestic things, in a way I never thought I would.

For many men learning to cope with domestic routine and manage that part of their lives is a source of considerable pride and self-respect. Getting some order into your life is a healthy and healing process. Mastering new domestic skills – even if it takes some swallowing of pride and some defiance of macho stereotypes to do it – is an excellent tonic for the ego.

For the male parent, whether custodial parent or not, roles and relationships with children can change dramatically after separation. Many of those changes will be for the better and even some which might appear at first to be problems can, if confronted positively, lead to a deeper and improved relationship between father and child.

Fathers must accept responsibility for defining their own relationship with their children rather than let their ex do the defining for them. They may have to do so initially in a relatively hostile environment or in one confused by their own emotional responses to their former partner. A simple rule of thumb is to put the new relationship – the one with the children – first and be clear about its importance.

Fathers who have the children living with them will probably have a whole range of new nurturing skills to master. Achieving this will mean dumping a great many traditional roles and prejudices. Many fathers, having cast off their role of husband, are inclined to let go of their role as father as well. This pattern may have begun during the first stages of the marriage breakdown – it may even have been one of its causes. Whatever, becoming a single father is a matter of positive choice. It is not something that can be left to chance. The more the single father willingly accepts all the responsibilities of his role – domestic and emotional – the more rewarding it is likely to be. Part of that acceptance is knowing the limitations of single-sex parenting and allowing as much input from the mother as she is willing to give and as the children need.

There may even be a time when, painful or not, a single father might have to accept that his custody is less helpful to that stage of a child's growth than its mother's. There is nothing inevitable about this, of course, and there is no legal, emotional or practical reason why a man should not be as capable of fulfilling the role of solo parent as can a woman. It is all a matter of choice.

It was obvious that in her new life she wasn't going to have room for our children. I didn't mind that in general, but I did worry about our daughter and how I would cope with providing her with the kind of role model an adolescent girl would need. After a bit of a rough start we coped quite well. If I accepted that I was the nurturing one and behaved accordingly she accepted me in that role. The important thing was to learn to listen to her and what she needed. I had to recognise I couldn't know all that by instinct and, after all, it was her needs that had to be met.

It was all a bit of an adventure at first. I loved baching with my son and he wasn't a bad kid and mucked in. But soon, what had started as fun became dreary routine and we let a lot of things slip. We hated it – messy house, a constant diet of takeaways, endless rows about who was going to do what. Then one Saturday after an awful row about something silly like hanging out the washing we sat down and talked it through. We did deals about how we could have a better life and worked out routines. I realised that the fault was not by any means one-sided and so did he. After that it got steadily better and we became very houseproud and keen to show each other how well we could cook this and that. Now that was a long time ago. He is a young man gone flatting and looking after himself in a way his mates envy. I learnt a lot too and I enjoy the single life because thanks to our experience of living together and caring for each other, I learnt how to make its trivial irritations seem pleasant and easy. The full-on experience of looking after a child growing into an adult makes looking after yourself a bit of a breeze.

Social expectations and male role pressures provide the separated man with a whole lot of obstacles he can do without. Dumping or ignoring them is an essential first step for a man becoming single. The first, hardest and most rewarding lesson for a man newly separated to learn is to go beyond his rage and injured pride, confront the pain behind it and come to terms with the reality of the process he has begun.

I've learnt so much. In the beginning I did everything wrong. I followed all the wrong instincts and took all the wrong advice, when I took any at all. But slowly it came right and I got through the other side. Would I go back? Well I suppose it was a love – a real love – that I will always regret losing, but no. No, I have come too far and made a life that in many ways is much, much richer than before. I have so much more of it in my control. I know so much more about myself. I don't rule out getting married again, but not as a half person any more — no way — and nor would I want to inflict that on anyone else. Next time it's as partners in the very best sense of that notion.

CHAPTER TWELVE

The Separated Woman

In 'The Rock', T.S. Eliot asks 'Where is the life we have lost in living? I remember those words returning to me when my husband left us. My life had been so used up living one way, living a life of compromise between putting aside a career in the outside world for a career rearing children and running a house. Perhaps those words had a certain relevance to my ex-husband, but for me, for a time, I felt completely adrift.

The change of status really affected my becoming single again. I could accept it all on the legal level, but the social implications took ages to work out. I didn't recognise for ages that I had to start behaving differently. I was out of the married's circle. I hated going to old friends alone and hearing their trivial problems. It was terrible not having anyone to confide in, who could help.

. . . .

No matter who leaves the marriage, it is likely to be the woman who suffers the most obvious emotional, social and financial impact. The 1980s have witnessed major and rapid changes in many areas of people's lives. A combination of economic and social pressures have propelled large numbers of women back into paid employment. More women have to work and more women have to support their families.

Stresses on marriages are probably greater than at any time since World War II, and while stresses on men and women may produce similar symptoms such as insomnia, depression and anxiety, in women the processes of menstruation, pregnancy and menopause add a heavy hormonal overlay to these problems. Hormones can play havoc with mental and physical health during times of great stress.

Most women experience upheavals in their menstrual cycles, which may become wildly erratic or prolonged. As mind and body recover their equilibrium these wild changes will also settle, but always check with your doctor if you are concerned.

I remember some time ago my ex-husband was having stress-related symptoms, when he was having a hard time at work. He went to the doctor for a check-up. He was given batteries of tests and was taken very seriously. Yet recently, when I started to crack-up after we separated, I'd been bleeding for over three months almost non-stop. My doctor said 'Don't worry dear, it just stress. Try to relax a bit more,' and prescribed some tranquillisers.

Reassurance that your physical symptoms are not terminal may be all you should expect from a busy family doctor. If your doctor is not able to offer the advice you think you need, then seek help elsewhere. Do not be put down or put off. Talk to friends. Most libraries have excellent books on women's health, written by women for women. Getting in contact with women's health clinics can put you in touch with people who have the time, interest and sympathy to help you sort out your problems.

Women approaching, or in the throes of, menopause face not only the tidal sweeps of erratic hormones, but the prospect of ageing and of 'being over the hill' in an age obsessed with youth and beauty. Facing this, while adapting to life alone, can lead to serious depression. It may seem cold comfort to remind yourself, if this is the reality that confronts you, that it is reality and that it is fruitless to yearn to be something you are not, or to mourn lost youth. Those feelings are natural ones, of course, but when you are adjusting to separation, with all its feelings of failure and rejection, it is not a particularly sensible time to indulge them. Try to catalogue, instead, all the things about yourself and your life that you know are achievements, that are positive and that please you.

Someone once told me that, for a woman, coming out of more than fifteen years of marriage was like coming out of prison. How unprepared you are for life on the 'outside'. The bust-up of my marriage happened when I was 49 and in the throes of a gaudy menopause. My youngest teenager had flown the nest. I couldn't believe how much I missed her bright young presence. My parents were becoming a bit shaky and demanded more of my time and my husband was having a slight crisis of his own in the form or a pneumatic popsy at work.

He couldn't cope and fled. I really don't know how I survived. I did though. In fact I did more than survive. I emerged from that time of hellfire a much stronger, self-reliant and self-confident woman. With help. Lots and lots of help.

Not all women's depressive illnesses can be blamed on hormones and the 'pecularities of her sex'. Hormonal imbalances are often the result of problems rather than the cause. Depression has been described as women's number one health problem. Most depression evolves out of women's feelings of social isolation, having no-one to confide in, living in situations over which they have no control and having problems they feel powerless to change.

As women over the last generation have faced more pressures and demanded and achieved more self-determination they have also developed support strategies specially related to women's problems. There are numerous women's groups which can advise and help women cope with almost every kind of problem from childcare to self-defence. A citizens' advice bureau or your local library will have a directory of those groups active in your area.

Media prejudice has made many women feel wary about women's groups. Much of that prejudice is based on male fears of female independence. Commonsense should tell you that women's groups are more likely to by sympathetic and relevant to women's problems than outdated institutions that may only reflect stereotyped attitudes.

I didn't know I was depressed. I didn't feel listless, or down, just anxious and guilty all the time – totally worthless. I didn't like myself very much and, what was worse, I didn't think I deserved any help and that somehow it was all my fault. So much of my life was based on fear. Fear of not being pretty enough. Fear of not pleasing my parents. Fear of not marrying. Then being held by fear to my husband, who threatened if I so much as looked at another man, that'd be the end. When I said 'I love you' to my husband, I was really saying 'I am afraid of you'.

Depression is a natural enough response to a failed marriage or broken relationship. It is important not to feel guilty or anxious about feeling that way. It is also important to believe that your depression will lift and that it is not a chronic state you will have to suffer forever.

Internalising anger and pain seems to be a much more common pattern in women than in men and finding outlets for these feelings can be difficult for many women. With greater separations from family roots and, perhaps, religious structures, many women find that they have no-one in particular to turn to.

I became a course junkie for a while. First I did re-birthing, then an anger resolution weekend and on to self-transformation. The feeling of being part of a group – I suppose my parents would have found it in church – was so revitalising. I think the thing about seeking help is how much it speeds up the healing process. I would have recovered eventually, maybe with a lot of unresolved conflict and maybe not, but I feel I have a backstop now, a refuge if the going gets too tough.

Help is available too for problems on a more practical level, for taking the stress out of learning about home finance and management, car maintenance and all those other things that might have fallen into the realm of the other half of the couple.

As a single woman you will need to develop your own financial profile. Taking out a hire purchase agreement on a small item and paying it off in time in the set instalments will give you a good credit rating for loans or hire purchase you may need in the future. It may seem odd, but to establish yourself as a good credit risk you have had to owe money – this may have been part of your family finances managed by your husband and you might find that your family credit rating has left with him.

If you have had joint bank accounts or joint debts or mortgages make sure that the liability for these is sorted out just as soon as you can cope. Explain your new situation to your bank manager. Get advice on money matters before problems arise and make sure you have a clear understanding of your economic situation. It may be grim, but it will certainly become a great deal grimmer if you let it get out of control.

While it may seem a great treat to be offered higher loan facilities on your credit card don't be tempted to accept credit of any kind unless you have a clear view of how you will manage your liabilities in the longer term. Accepting emergency help is a far cry from locking yourself into a future cycle of debt that you will have no chance of managing. If you have trouble balancing the domestic budget then ask at a citizens' advice bureau about voluntary agencies which can provide family budgeting help.

I lied for months about why I was going back to work, where my husband had gone and why my daughter had changed to a state school. Of course all my friends knew what was happening. A couple of them had joined the 'nouveau poor' too. You really do get an enormous boost to your self-esteem when you can successfully take control of the financial side of your life. I'd been brought up to think that money was a pretty vulgar topic, but in fact it's quite fascinating.

Women who left school with the 'career' plan of doing any old job until marriage and motherhood, find that the only jobs they are qualified for are low paid, low status ones. In bigger centres there are many options open to women to train for new careers. Adult education, technical institute and university extension centres run courses for women at this turning point in their lives. They also provide information networks that can open doors to all sorts of opportunities and alternatives. Some employment agencies specialise in helping women assess their skills and find suitable jobs.

I had been pretty depressed after trying tentatively on my own to find a job. I was in my mid-forties and hadn't had a job for about 15 years. I went to this agency and filled out forms. Actually I could only fill out one bit in the whole questionnaire! But the women assigned to me took me through it again and got me to mention all the volunteer jobs I had done, like play centre training and terms as secretary on the school committee. She pointed out that all work experience is valuable. I was given lots of advice on how to handle job interviews and how to dress. You've no idea how much help it was. It gave me so much confidence and put me in touch again.

If it is possible to buy time to further your education, retrain or attend courses that put you in contact with what's new, do not feel guilty about delaying going back to work. Many women have used to great advantage time spent to prepare for a fulfilling career. For women who put aside professional careers for marriage and motherhood, refresher courses are often a prerequisite for re-entry.

Childcare is a major problem for working mothers, single or not. If you find it difficult, get into lobbying your local council, member of parliament and the management at your place of work for childcare facilities and allowances. Make sure your union is active about the subject and lobby your local branch if it is not. A generation ago, women were virtually unseen in top jobs simply because they were women. Now many more opportunities are there to go to the top on ability, but those changes will be lost to working mothers if a childcare infrastructure is not there to support them.

High unemployment has led to high levels of self-employment and this is an area many women on their own are finding a satisfying challenge. With cheaper, smaller new microtechnology more women are doing computer and business practice courses and turning their houses into 'techno-villas'. Crafts and other 'do-it-yourself' skills also offer opportunities to establish worthwhile home-based businesses.

It is only 150 years since working from home was the rule rather than the exception for women. I read a quote about guilds in pre-industrial Britain where a man was considered a fool if 'he married a woman who could not support herself or her offspring'. We seem to have come the full circle in the late eighties.

For many women the two years from the time of separation to the final dissolution of the marriage can be just a grey limbo of not being quite off with the old nor on with the new way of life. Use it creatively as a time for active recovery, reflection, planning and self-discovery. For some women, particularly those who went straight from home to marriage, it may be their first time they have had to consider and value their own separate identity.

Relationships may seem to define who you are and what your value and status is, but in the end it is your own individual worth and qualities that really establish your identity. As a single person re-establishing herself you have a unique opportunity to begin to grow again as an individual.

I feel I am part of a vanguard generation of women who are reaching their forties, have had control over their fertility as no other generation has before, who have had good educations, who are having to forge into uncharted social territories without religious or family guidelines, who are behaving in quite different ways from their mothers and grandmothers. The new way for women seems to be to strive for economic and emotional independence.

There are a lot of single women in your community leading rich, full and secure lives. They raise children, they pursue careers, they contribute to the arts and to the welfare and happiness of others around them. Many of them have unravelled the pain you are experiencing, have overcome the same feelings of futility, guilt or failure that you may have. They have taken and made something of the opportunities beginning again has given them.

There are also just as many who have gone through the painful process of breaking up, have been strengthened by it and who now enjoy happier new relationships and marriages.

I spent the first few months on my own in a state of terror and anxiety. Lots of impotent rage too. I knew my husband wanted to marry again as soon as the divorce was through and I couldn't bear the though of being the 'first Mrs B' so I changed back to my single name. You don't even have to go to court – just reclaim it. It was odd how good it made me feel. As if I had claimed some of my life back too. I thought the kids might mind, but they thought it was fabulously modern. A real turning point.

I flailed about for years, finding a way of acting for myself, shrugging off 2000 years of cultural conditioning that I needed protection and to be dependent on a man for my existence. I can and do support myself and any relationships I do have with new men are a bonus and a delight rather than the reason for my being. It is important to see things as they are, not 'were' and 'should be'. God how I hate that phrase 'should be'.

CHAPTER THIRTEEN

Becoming Single

There are no celebrations at the end of a marriage, just a dry and formal pronouncement in court that the law is satisfied that it has ended. A relationship that was not a marriage can have an even more insubstantial ending than that. Yet the final act of breaking up a relationship is surely as important as its beginning. Very few who have gone through this process would not see it as a milestone.

All the other major events in our lives have their rituals – established social customs that help us through our grief, endorse our happiness or mark some moment in our life as extraordinary. Divorce and separation have none of those.

One reason for the lack of ritual to mark the end of a marriage or other committed relationship, is that society has only relatively recently acknowledged that such endings or such relationships outside marriage should be a normal part of human affairs.

For nearly 2000 years in western society, marriage was structured as a lifetime commitment – for better or for worse

– with divorce either totally prohibited, or so hedged about with religious, economic or social prohibitions, that it was available only to a select or very courageous few. Other forms of relationship were either prohibited or, if socially accepted, given little status within any religious or legal framework.

For the majority of our grandparents a failed marriage was a life sentence. Divorce was a social stigma few of them would willingly carry. In 1936 Edward VIII of England had no choice but to abdicate his throne or give up his plan to marry the twice-divorced Wallis Simpson.

Twenty years later, his niece, Princess Margaret, was obliged to renounce a divorced man she had fallen in love with. Yet only twenty years after that she was able to divorce the Earl of Snowdon with little public or official outrage.

When my marriage began to go wrong I remembered, with chilling clarity, the unhappiness of my own parents – their awful rows, the grim silences and the terrible feeling that they only endured this for the sake of myself and my sisters. My father is long dead and to bring up the subject of my own problems I asked my mother if things had really been as dreadful as they seemed. She said that there had been times which were really bad, but she and Dad were married and that was that. They just had to see it through.

My wife and I decided to tell our respective parents that we were separating and wanted to divorce. It was like confessing to some social disease. My mother just blurted out 'we have never had a divorce in this family' and refused to discuss it any further. Her parents weren't quite so blunt, but I could see that they thought divorce was the bad end my wife deserved for marrying a hopeless case like me.

Opposition to attempts to reform divorce laws in recent times often took the form of dismissing reasonable divorce laws as a Casanova's or Jezebel's charter – giving licence to bored or immoral husbands and wives itching to trade in their old spouse for a newer model. Divorce was seen as a frontal attack on the 'sacred institution of marriage and the family'.

In fact, the reality of divorce is that marriage is a sham institution without it. Even in the conservative climate of Cromwell's England, John Milton could write of divorce as a 'means of preserving peace in marriage and quiet in the family'.

In any reasonable society, divorce should represent the other side of the marital coin. The one institution survives as a reasonable choice by virtue of the other. Marriage should not be an institution as rigorous as some holy order, to which a man and woman are obliged to commit themselves for life by unbreakable vows. The decisions that ordinary people would need to make to be certain of such an arrangement are beyond most of us.

Mobility, increases in life expectancy, decreases in infant mortality, safe and readily available contraception, career opportunities for women and some breaking down of male stereotypes are just some of the changes in modern society that force a redefinition of the nature of marriage.

Our family is full of remarriages, de factos and other variations on the theme. At my father's funeral recently I couldn't help but be amazed at the huge crowd we had become. My ex-wife, her boyfriend, his children, our children, my sisters, brothers, new and old sisters and brothers-in-law. We're all terrifically bonded by affection for each other. We seem to be a new sort of urban tribe. This is our way of stemming the tide of isolation of those post-nuclear times and the loneliness and stress that goes with it.

Nothing could be a greater attack on marriage, or the family, than men and women forced to endure together a lifetime of incompatibility. Human emotions are fleeting. Love can endure for a lifetime or it can vanish in a matter of months or years. The quality of the emotion is not enhanced or debased by the length of time it survives.

The passionate love that began a relationship can evolve into a loving, lifetime partnership, or it can completely evaporate leaving two baffled people wondering how they got to where they are in their lives. More often than not the negative changes are sometimes experienced by only one partner or, at least, only recognised by one and the ending of the relationship is traumatic – the process described in the first part of this book.

It is also true that, for most of us, our social and emotional education is sadly deficient. Many marry or enter into committed relationships for the wrong reasons – a misreading of their emotions or obligations or, even, simply to find solace for emotional pain or deprivation elsewhere in their lives. Some people marry long before they should and then develop in a completely different direction, leaving their partner somewhere else.

Whatever the reason for its demise, once a relationship has ended no-one should be forced to continue in it. Rage as we might against the pain of breaking up, in the end our recovery will rely on our first accepting the reality of our separation, going as best we can through the process of grieving and, finally, letting go of the relationship.

Divorce, in itself, is not the last act of this particular drama in our lives. It is merely the legal recognition of the ending, by mutual consent or otherwise, of a contract. The real end comes when we finally let go of the old love. A large part of that is a recognition of changes in ourselves – a realisation that some critical stage in our lives is completed and we have come out the other side a different person.

Whether or not those changes are for the better is entirely up to us. The perhaps unasked for freedom of separation has presented us with challenges and opportunities we might otherwise not have had. A lot of those are about our personal growth. The last part of the process is when choices about ourselves become a priority and they are choices leading to changes that only we can make.

That is why we have called this book 'Becoming Single'.

Throughout the whole sorry business I saw very little of my ex-wife. I veered from blotting her out with hatred or just ignoring her existence. It was hard on me – self-inflicted, but I couldn't do anything else – and it was harder on the children who had to acquire diplomatic skills far beyond their years. Gradually I found my feet and found that my own life, right then and there, was a damn sight more interesting than my boring misery (yes, it even bored me by then). In fact, interesting is only half of it. Almost every day I found out things about myself I hadn't bothered to take time over before – good things which pleased me and things I didn't like or which were unfair and which I could mostly change. Then I ran into my wife at a party – something I had taken pains to avoid up to then – and I felt nothing, just a polite interest in what she was up to. Like meeting an old friend I had drifted away from. In the general conversation, catching up with other friends neither of us had seen for a long time, I realised that I was actually living an interesting and happy life. As a bonus I also realised that I was having a lively conversation with my ex-wife – something there had not been much of in the last years of our marriage.

Letting go does not necessarily mean blotting out the past and suppressing its experiences, happy or sad. It means a changed relationship with those past events; assessing them for what they are worth in a positive sense and for what they can add to your present and future life. Many people are tempted to cling to grief and sadness because those emotions may seem the strongest they have had. The experience of them may also have attracted a level of attention and sympathy the person had not experienced before. Sometimes tragic experiences are relived, over and over, as a means of avoiding the reality of the present and as an excuse for not doing anything about it.

Once when I was really down and feeling immensely sorry for myself I met this very wise woman at a party. Of course the conversation was all about me and how bloody awful I felt and how badly I had been treated. She countered every twist and turn I made away from the real issue – that it was I who was doing the feeling and the hurting and that it was I who could just as easily put an end to it. The effective thing about her advice was that she didn't say I couldn't or shouldn't feel the pain and rage, but that I should just feel those things in their proper measure and not install a negative emotion permanently in the driving seat of my mind.

One day a friend came to my place in tears. His pain and anguish billowed around my kitchen and I knew I reached a steady equilibrium at last when I could help and counsel him, with the memory of my own grief and anxiety firmly behind me and under control.

As we pointed out in the first two chapters of this book, separation is a process almost identical to that of bereavement. It has a beginning, a middle, and an end. Cling on to the middle and you can almost guarantee a life of pointless misery or fruitless bitterness. Sooner or later some light will dawn. You will realise that you cannot reverse the clock and change the separation, but you can change yourself. That process is challenging and exciting. The exciting, optimistic moments will come and go, of course, but eventually optimism will outweigh the doubts and the moments of black despair will become fewer.

Many people cannot face the challenges involved in the process of becoming single and hurl themselves into another relationship as soon as they can. Some may end up perfectly happy as a result, but many others will have simply repeated their earlier mistakes or they may only be able to make the new relationship work by suppressing the things they should have come to terms with in the old.

Becoming single does not mean a commitment to a life lived alone – although for some people it may – it simply means becoming a whole person. Emerging from the other side of separation feeling stronger and more confident is a commonly reported experience. Deep in the throes of the pain it may not seem like that, but a majority of people do feel they have achieved some quite unexpected goals by going through the process.

I had a small afternoon party just for my women friends. I'd done a massive clean-up of my flat and filled the vases with fresh flowers. All my friends brought food or a bottle. The talk was pretty predictable – optimism at first, then after a few drinks out with the knives for specific men, men in general, then the government, the world. Then more drinks. Music, jokes and finally, toasts – to new beginnings. After, we all tottered off to dinner with husbands, lovers, new friends. Hope runs eternal doesn't it and 'our Father's (in my case my Mother's) house has many mansions'.

It has taken me a long time. Nearly four years. I suppose that's not too much after 18 years of marriage. Anyway I thought I would never get over it. Not ever. I won't say I haven't got the scars still, or that they are going to vanish, or that I'm not going to carry a bit of grief, a bit of pain and stuff right through to the end of my life. But the important thing is that it is a very different life. More positive. More defined. More certain in a lot of ways. And bits of me are a lot softer. I feel more tender towards people than I ever remember before and I'm not afraid to show friends how I feel, and I can genuinely say that I love my friends without any inhibition – men friends and women friends, although I have more of the latter because having gone through the fire and having had that fire change my life I don't relate too well to other men who are stuck in their hardcase shells. It's really funny to reflect that you can get to nearly fifty before you know you have grown up at last. Even better, I did it as a person alone, not as half a person. So many ordinary things in my life seem richer. I don't mean richer materially, but more marked by me. The way I live. I don't live any longer in borrowed clothes and, like it or not, what you see is what you get.